Level B

Mastering Math

Program Consultants

Robert Abbott
Assistant Director of Special Education
Waukegan Community Unit School District No. 60
Waukegan, Illinois

Marie Davis
Principal, McCoy Elementary School
Orange County Public Schools
Orlando, Florida

Monika Spindel
Mathematics Teacher
Austin, Texas

Suzanne H. Stevens
Specialist in Learning Disabilities
Learning Enhancement Consultant
Winston-Salem, North Carolina

STECK-VAUGHN
ELEMENTARY · SECONDARY · ADULT · LIBRARY

A Harcourt Company

www.steck-vaughn.com

Table of Contents

Acknowledgments

Editorial Director
Diane Schnell

Supervising Editor
Donna Rodgers

Assistant Art Director
Cynthia Ellis

Design Manager
Sheryl Cota

Media Researcher
Claudette Landry

Contributing Writers
Brantley Eastman, Diane Crowley, Mary Hill, Louise Marinilli, Harriet Stevens, Susan Murphy, Helen Coleman, Ann McSweeney

Illustration
Elizabeth Allen: pages 4, 8, 13, 34, 35, 47, 51, 54, 59, 84, 101, 127, 132, 133, 157   Ben Anglin: pages 9, 46, 48, 50, 76, 94, 105, 142   Ruth Brunke: pages T20, T24, T31, 3, 6, 10, 11, 15, 24, 25, 29, 33, 37, 40, 43, 53, 56, 57, 70, 78, 82, 86, 87, 89, 103, 111, 137, 145, 149   Holly Cooper: page 123   Laura Jackson: pages 52, 94   Rich Lo: money   Jimmy Longacre: pages 12, 61, 66, 77, 80, 81, 83, 85, 91, 96, 112, 134, 148, 152, 154, 157   Lynn McClain: page 2

Photography
Cover: (bug) ©Stockbyte; pp. 1, 23 ©PhotoDisc; p. 45 ©Michael Keller/The Stock Market; p. 55 ©PhotoDisc, p. 75 ©Chuck Savage/The Stock Market; p. 97 ©PhotoDisc; p. 99 ©Jon Feingersh/The Stock Market; p. 107 ©PhotoDisc; p. 119 ©Superstock; p. 121 ©PhotoDisc; Additional photography by: Digital Studios.

Cover Design
Tocquigny Design, Inc.

ISBN 0-7398-1245-9

Addition and Subtraction Facts Through 10

Tim uses 5 crayons.
Kim uses 4 crayons.
How many crayons
in all do they use?

Solve

▷ Write a problem to add or subtract crayons.

Adding to 6

How many  in all?

Add.

$$\begin{array}{r} 2 \\ + 4 \\ \hline 6 \end{array}$$
↑
sum

 in all.

Guided Practice

▶ Add.

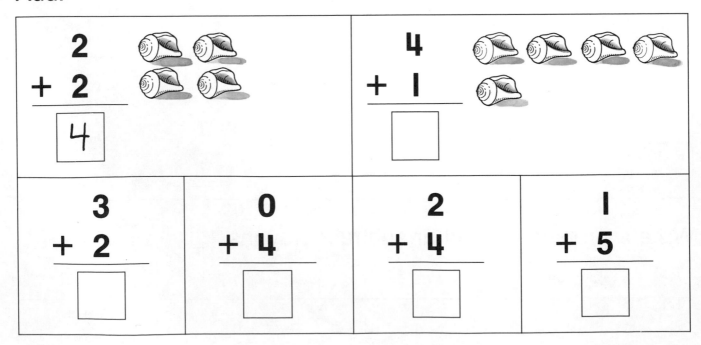

$$\begin{array}{r} 2 \\ + 2 \\ \hline \boxed{4} \end{array}$$

$$\begin{array}{r} 4 \\ + 1 \\ \hline \end{array}$$

$$\begin{array}{r} 3 \\ + 2 \\ \hline \end{array}$$

$$\begin{array}{r} 0 \\ + 4 \\ \hline \end{array}$$

$$\begin{array}{r} 2 \\ + 4 \\ \hline \end{array}$$

$$\begin{array}{r} 1 \\ + 5 \\ \hline \end{array}$$

Practice

▶Add.

1. $\begin{array}{r} 1 \\ +\ 0 \\ \hline \square \end{array}$	2. $\begin{array}{r} 2 \\ +\ 1 \\ \hline \square \end{array}$	3. $\begin{array}{r} 3 \\ +\ 3 \\ \hline \square \end{array}$	4. $\begin{array}{r} 4 \\ +\ 2 \\ \hline \square \end{array}$
5. $\begin{array}{r} 1 \\ +\ 1 \\ \hline \square \end{array}$	6. $\begin{array}{r} 1 \\ +\ 5 \\ \hline \square \end{array}$	7. $\begin{array}{r} 3 \\ +\ 1 \\ \hline \square \end{array}$	8. $\begin{array}{r} 0 \\ +\ 5 \\ \hline \square \end{array}$
9. $\begin{array}{r} 1 \\ +\ 4 \\ \hline \square \end{array}$	10. $\begin{array}{r} 2 \\ +\ 2 \\ \hline \square \end{array}$	11. $\begin{array}{r} 2 \\ +\ 3 \\ \hline \square \end{array}$	12. $\begin{array}{r} 6 \\ +\ 0 \\ \hline \square \end{array}$

Using Math

▶How many 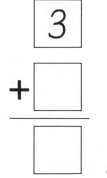 in all?

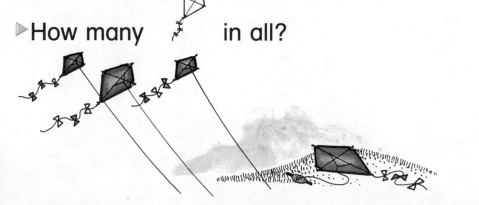

$\begin{array}{r} 3 \\ +\ \square \\ \hline \square \end{array}$ 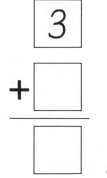 in all.

3

Adding to 8

How many 🖍 in all?

Add.

$$
\begin{array}{r}
6 \\
+\ 2 \\
\hline
8
\end{array}
$$
🖍 in all.

Guided Practice

▷ Add.

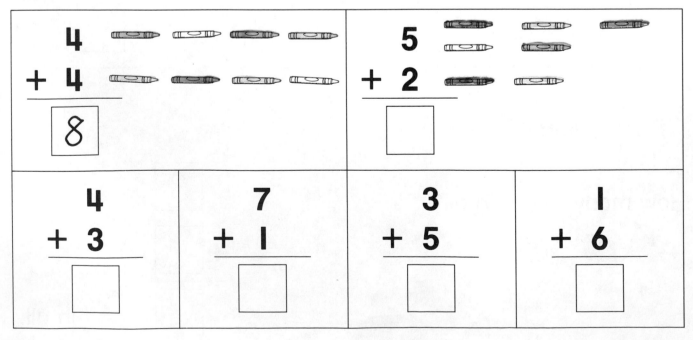

$$
\begin{array}{r}
4 \\
+\ 4 \\
\hline
8
\end{array}
$$

$$
\begin{array}{r}
5 \\
+\ 2 \\
\hline

\end{array}
$$

$$
\begin{array}{r}
4 \\
+\ 3 \\
\hline

\end{array}
$$

$$
\begin{array}{r}
7 \\
+\ 1 \\
\hline

\end{array}
$$

$$
\begin{array}{r}
3 \\
+\ 5 \\
\hline

\end{array}
$$

$$
\begin{array}{r}
1 \\
+\ 6 \\
\hline

\end{array}
$$

Practice

▷ Add.

1. 4 + 1 □	2. 7 + 0 □	3. 3 + 3 □	4. 1 + 7 □
5. 0 + 6 □	6. 2 + 3 □	7. 6 + 1 □	8. 2 + 6 □
9. 5 + 2 □	10. 2 + 4 □	11. 3 + 4 □	12. 0 + 8 □

Using Math

▷ How many  in all?

in all.

5

Adding to 10

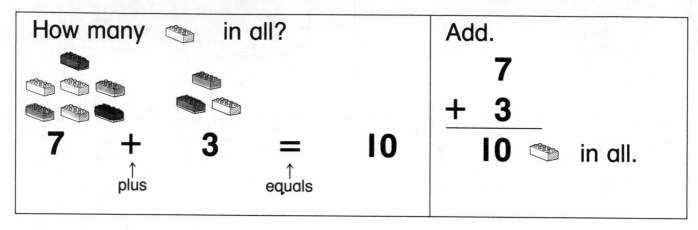

How many in all?

7   +   3   =   10

        ↑   ↑
      plus   equals

Add.

$$\begin{array}{r} 7 \\ + \ 3 \\ \hline 10 \end{array}$$ in all.

Guided Practice

▷ Add.

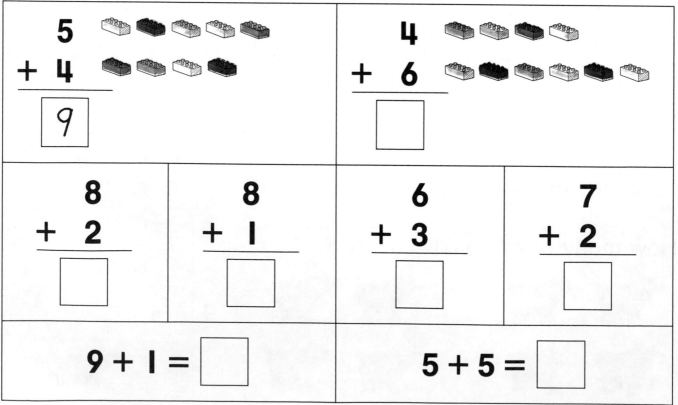

$$\begin{array}{r} 5 \\ + \ 4 \\ \hline \boxed{9} \end{array}$$

$$\begin{array}{r} 4 \\ + \ 6 \\ \hline \ \ \square \end{array}$$

$$\begin{array}{r} 8 \\ + \ 2 \\ \hline \ \ \square \end{array}$$

$$\begin{array}{r} 8 \\ + \ 1 \\ \hline \ \ \square \end{array}$$

$$\begin{array}{r} 6 \\ + \ 3 \\ \hline \ \ \square \end{array}$$

$$\begin{array}{r} 7 \\ + \ 2 \\ \hline \ \ \square \end{array}$$

9 + 1 = $\square$ 5 + 5 = $\square$

Practice

▷ Add.

1. $\begin{array}{r} 4 \\ + 4 \\ \hline \end{array}$	2. $\begin{array}{r} 2 \\ + 8 \\ \hline \end{array}$	3. $\begin{array}{r} 3 \\ + 6 \\ \hline \end{array}$	4. $\begin{array}{r} 0 \\ + 9 \\ \hline \end{array}$
5. $\begin{array}{r} 7 \\ + 3 \\ \hline \end{array}$	6. $\begin{array}{r} 3 \\ + 4 \\ \hline \end{array}$	7. $\begin{array}{r} 5 \\ + 5 \\ \hline \end{array}$	8. $\begin{array}{r} 1 \\ + 8 \\ \hline \end{array}$

9. $6 + 4 = \boxed{}$ 10. $4 + 5 = \boxed{}$

11. $1 + 9 = \boxed{}$ 12. $2 + 7 = \boxed{}$

Using Math

▷ How many in all?

$\boxed{}$ + $\boxed{}$ = $\boxed{}$ in all.

7

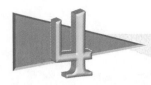

Subtraction Facts Through 6

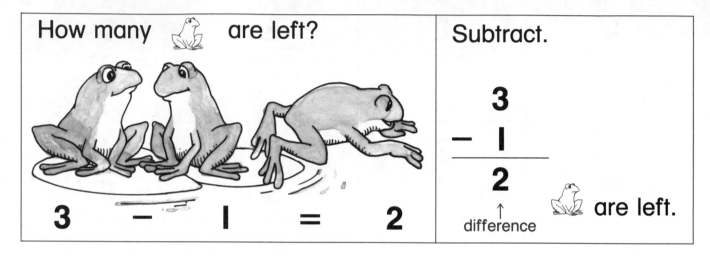

How many 🐸 are left?

3 − 1 = 2

Subtract.

$$\begin{array}{r} 3 \\ -\ 1 \\ \hline 2 \end{array}$$

↑
difference

🐸 are left.

Guided Practice

▷ Subtract.

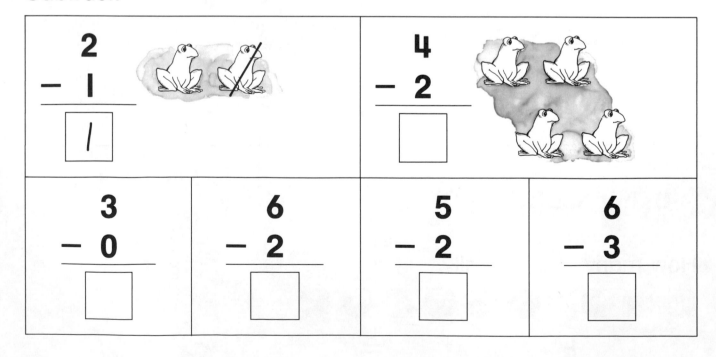

$$\begin{array}{r} 2 \\ -\ 1 \\ \hline \boxed{1} \end{array}$$

$$\begin{array}{r} 4 \\ -\ 2 \\ \hline \boxed{} \end{array}$$

$$\begin{array}{r} 3 \\ -\ 0 \\ \hline \boxed{} \end{array}$$

$$\begin{array}{r} 6 \\ -\ 2 \\ \hline \boxed{} \end{array}$$

$$\begin{array}{r} 5 \\ -\ 2 \\ \hline \boxed{} \end{array}$$

$$\begin{array}{r} 6 \\ -\ 3 \\ \hline \boxed{} \end{array}$$

Practice

▶Subtract.

1. $\begin{array}{r} 3 \\ -\ 2 \\ \hline \square \end{array}$	2. $\begin{array}{r} 4 \\ -\ 1 \\ \hline \square \end{array}$	3. $\begin{array}{r} 2 \\ -\ 2 \\ \hline \square \end{array}$	4. $\begin{array}{r} 5 \\ -\ 3 \\ \hline \square \end{array}$
5. $\begin{array}{r} 6 \\ -\ 1 \\ \hline \square \end{array}$	6. $\begin{array}{r} 5 \\ -\ 4 \\ \hline \square \end{array}$	7. $\begin{array}{r} 4 \\ -\ 0 \\ \hline \square \end{array}$	8. $\begin{array}{r} 3 \\ -\ 1 \\ \hline \square \end{array}$
9. $\begin{array}{r} 4 \\ -\ 4 \\ \hline \square \end{array}$	10. $\begin{array}{r} 6 \\ -\ 5 \\ \hline \square \end{array}$	11. $\begin{array}{r} 4 \\ -\ 2 \\ \hline \square \end{array}$	12. $\begin{array}{r} 6 \\ -\ 4 \\ \hline \square \end{array}$

Using Math

▶How many in all?

How many leave?

How many are left?

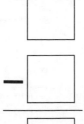

Subtracting from 7 and 8

How many 🐞 are left?

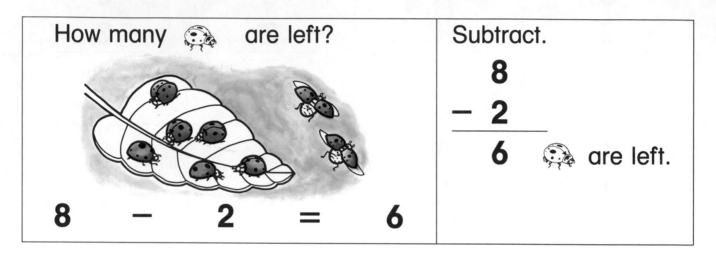

8   −   2   =   6

Subtract.

$$
\begin{array}{r}
8 \\
-\ 2 \\
\hline
6
\end{array}
$$
🐞 are left.

Guided Practice

▷ Subtract.

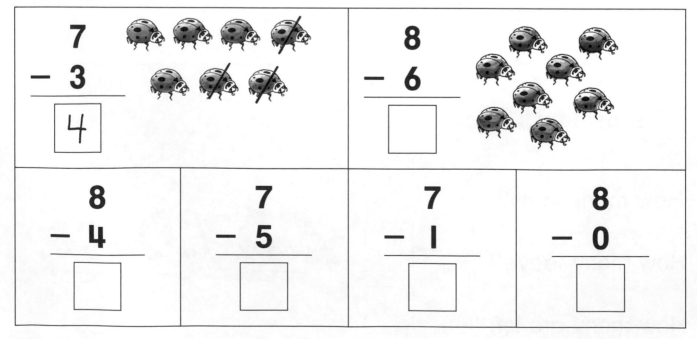

$$
\begin{array}{r}
7 \\
-\ 3 \\
\hline
\boxed{4}
\end{array}
$$

$$
\begin{array}{r}
8 \\
-\ 6 \\
\hline
\ \\
\end{array}
$$

$$
\begin{array}{r}
8 \\
-\ 4 \\
\hline
\ \\
\end{array}
$$

$$
\begin{array}{r}
7 \\
-\ 5 \\
\hline
\ \\
\end{array}
$$

$$
\begin{array}{r}
7 \\
-\ 1 \\
\hline
\ \\
\end{array}
$$

$$
\begin{array}{r}
8 \\
-\ 0 \\
\hline
\ \\
\end{array}
$$

10

Practice

▷Subtract.

1. $\begin{array}{r} 7 \\ -\ 0 \\ \hline \end{array}$	2. $\begin{array}{r} 8 \\ -\ 7 \\ \hline \end{array}$	3. $\begin{array}{r} 7 \\ -\ 4 \\ \hline \end{array}$	4. $\begin{array}{r} 6 \\ -\ 2 \\ \hline \end{array}$
5. $\begin{array}{r} 8 \\ -\ 5 \\ \hline \end{array}$	6. $\begin{array}{r} 7 \\ -\ 5 \\ \hline \end{array}$	7. $\begin{array}{r} 8 \\ -\ 6 \\ \hline \end{array}$	8. $\begin{array}{r} 8 \\ -\ 2 \\ \hline \end{array}$
9. $\begin{array}{r} 6 \\ -\ 3 \\ \hline \end{array}$	10. $\begin{array}{r} 7 \\ -\ 1 \\ \hline \end{array}$	11. $\begin{array}{r} 8 \\ -\ 4 \\ \hline \end{array}$	12. $\begin{array}{r} 8 \\ -\ 3 \\ \hline \end{array}$

Using Math

▷How many in all?

How many blew out?

How many are left?

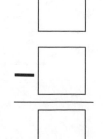

Subtracting from 9 and 10

How many  are left?

10   −   4   =   6

↑
minus

Subtract.

$$10 - 4 = 6$$ are left.

Guided Practice

▷ Subtract.

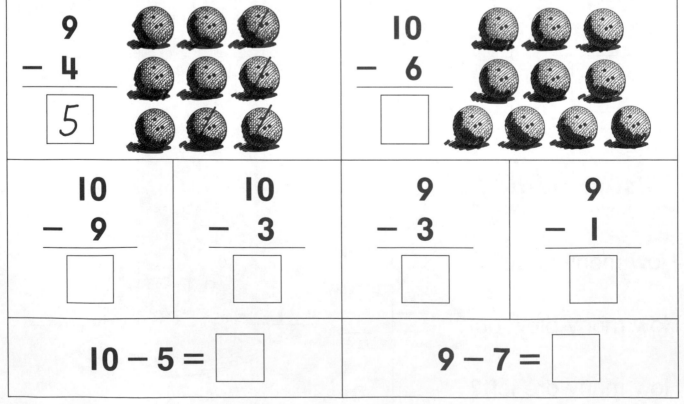

$$\begin{array}{r} 9 \\ -\ 4 \\ \hline \boxed{5} \end{array}$$

$$\begin{array}{r} 10 \\ -\ 6 \\ \hline \boxed{} \end{array}$$

$$\begin{array}{r} 10 \\ -\ 9 \\ \hline \boxed{} \end{array}$$

$$\begin{array}{r} 10 \\ -\ 3 \\ \hline \boxed{} \end{array}$$

$$\begin{array}{r} 9 \\ -\ 3 \\ \hline \boxed{} \end{array}$$

$$\begin{array}{r} 9 \\ -\ 1 \\ \hline \boxed{} \end{array}$$

$$10 - 5 = \boxed{}$$

$$9 - 7 = \boxed{}$$

Practice

▷ Subtract.

1. $\begin{array}{r} 9 \\ -\ 2 \\ \hline \end{array}$ ☐	**2.** $\begin{array}{r} 8 \\ -\ 3 \\ \hline \end{array}$ ☐	**3.** $\begin{array}{r} 10 \\ -\ 7 \\ \hline \end{array}$ ☐	**4.** $\begin{array}{r} 10 \\ -\ 4 \\ \hline \end{array}$ ☐
5. $\begin{array}{r} 9 \\ -\ 5 \\ \hline \end{array}$ ☐	**6.** $\begin{array}{r} 10 \\ -\ 8 \\ \hline \end{array}$ ☐	**7.** $\begin{array}{r} 10 \\ -\ 1 \\ \hline \end{array}$ ☐	**8.** $\begin{array}{r} 9 \\ -\ 6 \\ \hline \end{array}$ ☐

9. $10 - 0 =$ ☐

10. $9 - 8 =$ ☐

Using Math

▷ How many in all?

How many fall?

How many are left?

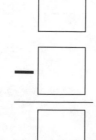

Pennies and Nickels

penny 1¢	penny 1¢	nickel 5¢	nickel 5¢

      =

Guided Practice

▶ How much money?

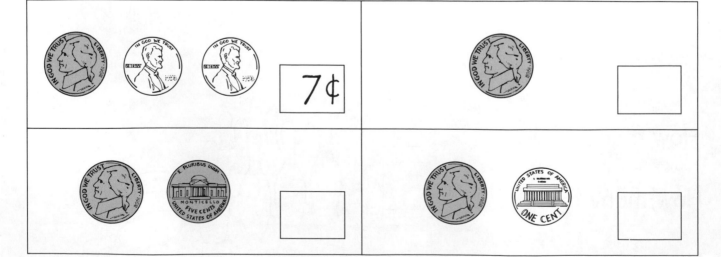

Practice

▷How much money?

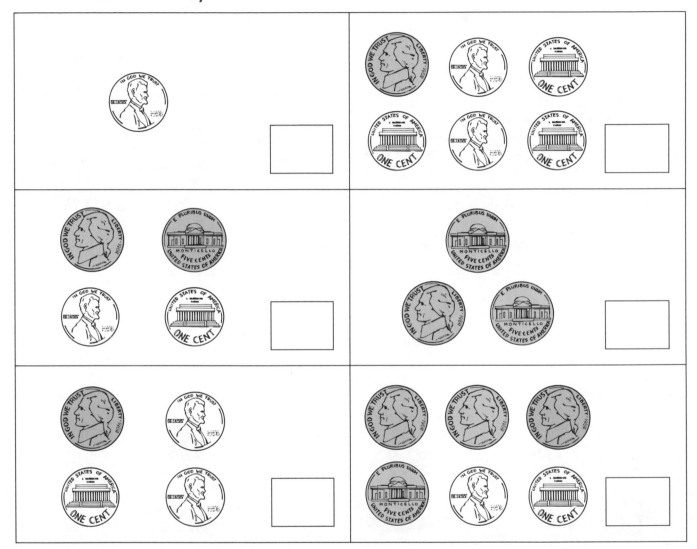

Using Math

▷Mark how much money.

Use a Picture

Guided Practice

▷ Count the pictures.
Write how many.

▷ Write how many.
Add.

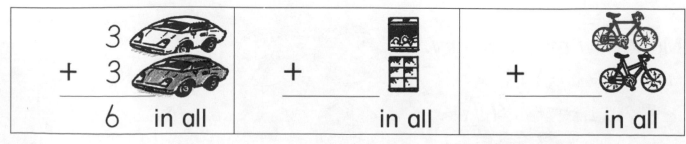

Practice

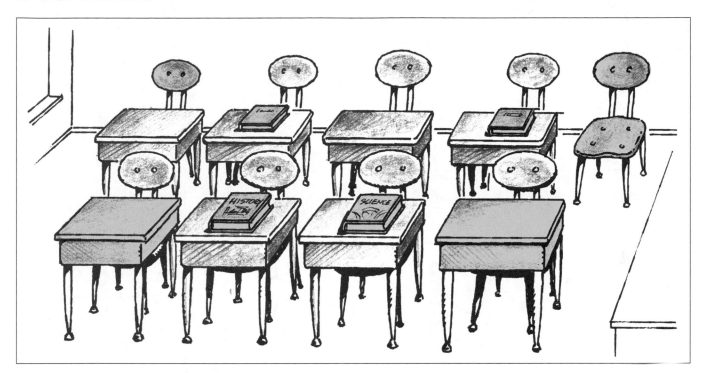

▷Count the pictures.
Write how many.

1.  _____	2. _____	3. _____
4. _____	5. _____	6. _____

▷Write how many.
Add.

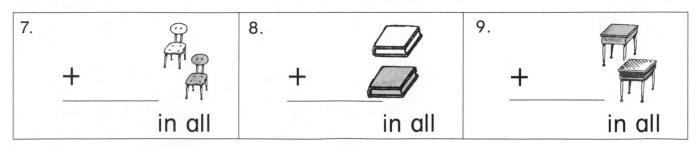

7.	8.	9.
+ _____	+ _____	+ _____
in all	in all	in all

▷ Add.

pages 2–3			
1. **2** **+ 2** ☐	2. **4** **+ 1** ☐	3. **3** **+ 2** ☐	4. **2** **+ 4** ☐
pages 4–5			
5. **3** **+ 4** ☐	6. **2** **+ 5** ☐	7. **4** **+ 4** ☐	8. **6** **+ 2** ☐

pages 6–7

9. $5 + 5 =$ ☐   10. $8 + 1 =$ ☐

11. $3 + 7 =$ ☐   12. $4 + 5 =$ ☐

▷ Subtract.

pages 8–9			
13. **3** **− 2** ☐	14. **5** **− 0** ☐	15. **6** **− 3** ☐	16. **4** **− 2** ☐

▶Subtract.

<table>
<tr><td>

pages 10–11

17. **8**
   − 4
   ☐

</td><td>

18. **7**
   − 5
   ☐

</td><td>

19. **8**
   − 2
   ☐

</td><td>

20. **7**
   − 3
   ☐

</td></tr>
</table>

pages 12–13

21. **9 − 3 =** ☐   22. **10 − 6 =** ☐

23. **9 − 7 =** ☐   24. **10 − 5 =** ☐

25. **10 − 9 =** ☐   26. **9 − 1 =** ☐

▶How much money?

pages 14–15

27.

  ☐

28.

    ☐

▷Count the pictures.

Write how many. pages 16–17

29. 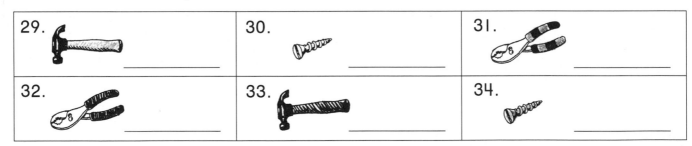	30.	31.
32.	33.	34.

▷Write how many.

Add.

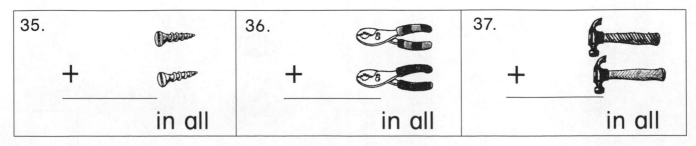

35.	36.	37.
+	+	+
in all	in all	in all

▷Add.

1. 1 + 3 ☐	2. 3 + 3 ☐	3. 2 + 6 ☐	4. 4 + 3 ☐

5. 3 + 5 = ☐	6. 9 + 0 = ☐	7. 6 + 4 = ☐

▷Subtract.

8. 4 − 3 ☐	9. 6 − 2 ☐	10. 5 − 1 ☐	11. 7 − 4 ☐

12. 8 − 6 = ☐	13. 10 − 7 = ☐	14. 9 − 4 = ☐

▷How much money?

15.   ☐

▷Count the pictures.

Write how many.

16.		17.		18.	
19.		20.		21.	

▷Write how many.

Add.

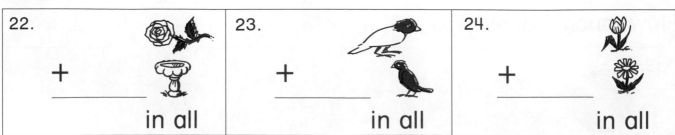

22. _____ in all	23. _____ in all	24. _____ in all

22

2 Place Value Through 999

▼ ▼ ▼ ▼ ▼ ▼ ▼

There are 97 penguins in all. How many tens and ones is this?

Solve

▷ Make up a problem using tens and ones.

11 Through 19

🍓🍓🍓🍓🍓 🍓🍓🍓🍓🍓 🍓 **11** eleven	🍓🍓🍓🍓🍓 🍓🍓🍓🍓🍓 🍓🍓 **12** twelve	🍓🍓🍓🍓🍓 🍓🍓🍓🍓🍓 🍓🍓🍓 **13** thirteen
🍓🍓🍓🍓🍓 🍓🍓🍓🍓🍓 🍓🍓🍓🍓 **14** fourteen	🍓🍓🍓🍓🍓 🍓🍓🍓🍓🍓 🍓🍓🍓🍓🍓 **15** fifteen	🍓🍓🍓🍓🍓 🍓🍓🍓🍓🍓 🍓🍓🍓🍓🍓 🍓 **16** sixteen
🍓🍓🍓🍓🍓 🍓🍓🍓🍓🍓 🍓🍓🍓🍓🍓 🍓🍓 **17** seventeen	🍓🍓🍓🍓🍓 🍓🍓🍓🍓🍓 🍓🍓🍓🍓🍓 🍓🍓🍓 **18** eighteen	🍓🍓🍓🍓🍓 🍓🍓🍓🍓🍓 🍓🍓🍓🍓🍓 🍓🍓🍓🍓 **19** nineteen

Guided Practice

▷ Write each number.

🥫🥫🥫🥫🥫 🥫🥫🥫🥫🥫🥫	eleven	**11**	
🥫🥫🥫🥫🥫🥫 🥫🥫🥫🥫🥫🥫🥫	thirteen		
🥫🥫🥫🥫🥫🥫 🥫🥫🥫🥫🥫🥫	twelve		
🥫🥫🥫🥫🥫 🥫🥫🥫🥫🥫🥫🥫 🥫🥫🥫🥫🥫 🥫🥫	nineteen		

Practice

▷Write each number.

1. 🍎🍎🍎🍎🍎🍎 🍎🍎🍎🍎 🍎🍎🍎🍎 **fourteen**	☐	2. 🍎🍎🍎🍎🍎 🍎🍎 🍎🍎🍎🍎🍎 🍎🍎🍎 **fifteen**	☐
3. 🍎🍎🍎🍎🍎 🍎🍎🍎 🍎🍎🍎🍎🍎 🍎🍎🍎 **sixteen**	☐	4. 🍎🍎🍎🍎🍎 🍎🍎🍎🍎 🍎🍎🍎🍎🍎 🍎🍎🍎🍎 **eighteen**	☐
5. 🍎🍎🍎🍎🍎 🍎🍎🍎🍎🍎 🍎 **eleven**	☐	6. 🍎🍎🍎🍎🍎 🍎🍎🍎🍎 🍎🍎🍎🍎🍎 🍎🍎🍎🍎🍎 **nineteen**	☐
7. 🍎🍎🍎🍎🍎 🍎🍎🍎 🍎🍎🍎🍎🍎 🍎🍎🍎🍎 **seventeen**	☐	8. 🍎🍎🍎🍎🍎 🍎 🍎🍎🍎🍎🍎 🍎🍎 **thirteen**	☐

Using Math

▷Pedro is **twelve** today.
Circle his age.

11   12   13   14   15

Tens and Ones to 19

Group 10 **ones** to make 1 **ten**.

□ □ □ □ □
□ □ □ □ □

10 ones = **1** ten

tens	ones		
1	5	=	15

Guided Practice

▷ Write how many.

tens	ones
1	2

= 12

tens	ones

=

tens	ones

=

tens	ones

=

Practice

▷Write how many.

1.	tens	ones		
	▯	▯	=	▢

2.	tens	ones		
	▯	▯ ▯ ▯ ▯ ▯ ▯ ▯ ▯	=	▢

3.	tens	ones		
	▯	▯ ▯ ▯ ▯ ▯	=	▢

4.	tens	ones		
	▯	▯ ▯	=	▢

Using Math

▷Ring 10  .

How many 🍎 are left? ▢

27

Counting Tens

Count tens.

1 ten = 10 ten	2 tens = 20 twenty	3 tens = 30 thirty
4 tens = 40 forty	5 tens = 50 fifty	6 tens = 60 sixty
7 tens = 70 seventy	8 tens = 80 eighty	9 tens = 90 ninety

Guided Practice

▷ Write each number.

2 tens = 20	4 tens = ☐	3 tens = ☐
5 tens = ☐	1 ten = ☐	9 tens = ☐

Practice

▷Write the number.

1. 4 tens = ☐	2. 1 ten = ☐
3. 7 tens = ☐	4. 2 tens = ☐
5. 8 tens = ☐	6. 5 tens = ☐
7. 6 tens = ☐	8. 9 tens = ☐

Using Math

▷Polly buys 3 🥚. Circle how many 🧁 in all.

20   30   40

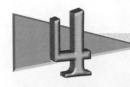

Tens and Ones to 99

tens	ones
▯▯▯	□
	□ □
	□ □
	□ □
3	7

= 37

37 = 3 tens 7 ones

Guided Practice

▶ Write how many tens and ones.

tens	ones
▯▯	□ □
	□ □
	□ □
2	6

26 = ⎡2⎤ tens ⎡6⎤ ones

tens	ones
▯▯▯▯	□ □ □
4	3

43 = ⎡ ⎤ tens ⎡ ⎤ ones

74 = ⎡ ⎤ tens ⎡ ⎤ ones

91 = ⎡ ⎤ tens ⎡ ⎤ one

Practice

▷Write how many tens and ones.

1. 32 = [ ] tens [ ] ones

2. 55 = [ ] tens [ ] ones

3. 40 = [ ] tens [ ] ones

4. 27 = [ ] tens [ ] ones

5. 76 = [ ] tens [ ] ones

6. 89 = [ ] tens [ ] ones

7. 11 = [ ] ten [ ] one

8. 95 = [ ] tens [ ] ones

Problem Solving

▷Write how many.
Add.

+ [ ]
___
[ ] in all

31

Hundreds, Tens, and Ones

You group numbers by hundreds, tens, and ones.

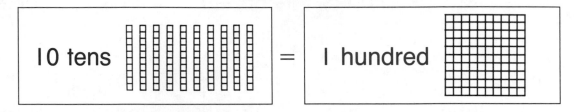

hundreds	tens	ones	
2	4	3	= 243

Guided Practice

▶ Write each number.

hundreds	tens	ones	
1	3	4	= 134

hundreds	tens	ones	
3	0	5	=

Practice

▷ Write each number.

1.	hundreds	tens	ones		
	3	I	9	=	

2.	hundreds	tens	ones		
	4	2	0	=	

3.	hundreds	tens	ones		
	6	3	4	=	

4.	hundreds	tens	ones		
	5	8	7	=	

5.	hundreds	tens	ones		
	7	0	3	=	

6.	hundreds	tens	ones		
	9	6	2	=	

Using Math

▷ The store has 324 🍒 .
Color how many.

hundreds	
tens	
ones	

Ordering Numbers to 999

You count numbers in order.

Ones	1	2	3	4	5	6	7	8	9
Tens	10	20	30	40	50	60	70	80	90
Hundreds	100	200	300	400	500	600	700	800	900

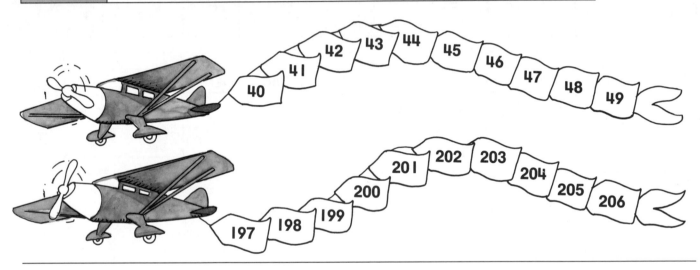

Guided Practice

▷ Write each missing number.

21	22	23	24	25

65	66		68	69

142	143		145	146

226		228	229	230

598	599		601	

810	811		813	

Practice

▶ Write each missing number.

1.
25	26		28

2.
30		32	33

3.
46		48	49

4.
58	59		61

5.
70	71		73

6.
102		104	105

7.
255		257	258

8.
583	584		

9.
743			746

10.
	997		999

Using Math

▶ Start with 100.
Connect the dots in order.

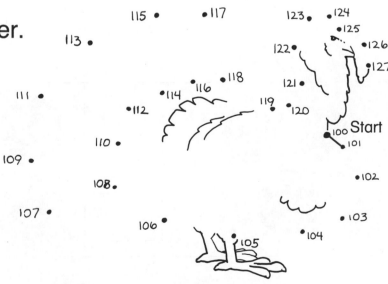

Dimes

dime 10¢	dime 10¢

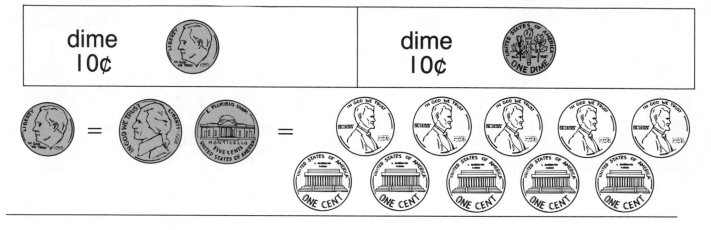

Guided Practice

▶How much money?

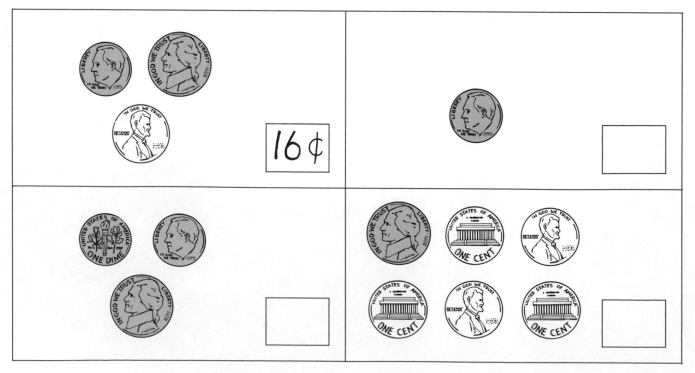

16¢

Practice

▷How much money?

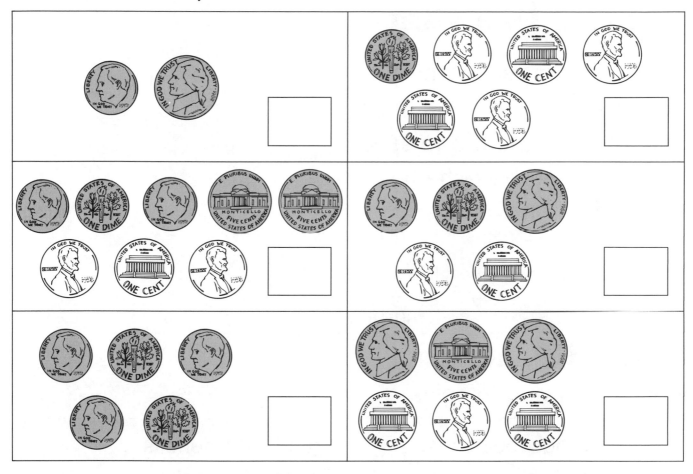

Using Math

▷Mark how much money.

37¢

Make a Drawing

Amy had 4 green marbles.

Ben gave her 3 more marbles.

Amy draws a picture to see

how many marbles she has now.

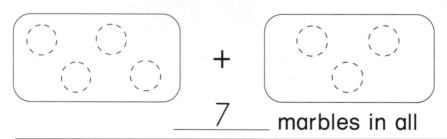

_____7_____ marbles in all

Guided Practice

▷Make a drawing to solve.

Jim had 5 baseball caps. Carlos has 4 baseball caps. How many do they have in all? ☐ + ☐ _____ baseball caps in all	Fran has 3 pencils. Tia has 6 pencils. How many do they have in all? ☐ + ☐ _____ pencils in all

Practice

▶Make a drawing to solve.

1. Lee has 2 apples.
   Sue has 2 apples.
   How many do they have
   in all?

   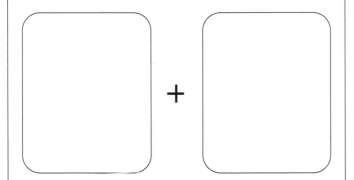

   _____ apples in all

2. Juan had 3 pennies.
   Dan gave him 4 more.
   How many does Juan have
   in all?

   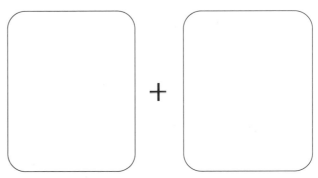

   _____ pennies in all

3. Jill had 7 pieces of gum.
   She bought 2 more pieces.
   How many does she have
   in all?

   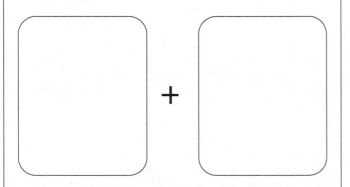

   _____ pieces of gum in all

4. Aldo had 5 fish.
   He bought 2 more fish.
   How many does he have
   in all?

   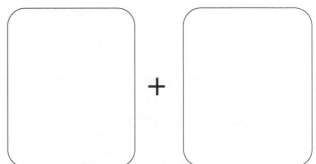

   _____ fish in all

▶ Write each number.
pages 24–25

1.	2.	3.
eleven ☐	seventeen ☐	fifteen ☐

▶ Write how many.
pages 26–27

4.

tens	ones

= ☐

5.

tens	ones

=

▶ Write each number.
pages 28–29

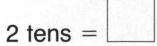

6.	7.	8.
2 tens = ☐	5 tens = ☐	8 tens = ☐

▶Write how many tens and ones.
pages 30–31

9.	10.
34 = ☐ tens ☐ ones	90 = ☐ tens ☐ ones

▶Write each number.
pages 32–33

11.

hundreds	tens	ones
1	2	5

= ☐

12.

hundreds	tens	ones
7	6	2

= ☐

13.

hundreds	tens	ones
3	9	4

= ☐

14.

hundreds	tens	ones
8	5	0

= ☐

▶Write each missing number. pages 34–35

15.

32		34	35

16.

698		700	701

▶How much money?
pages 36–37

17.

    ☐

18.

   ☐

▶**Make a drawing to solve.** pages 38–39

19. Tony made 4 pictures.
Glenn made 4 pictures.
How many did they have
in all?

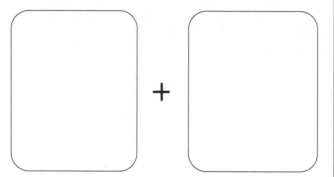

_____ pictures in all

20. Saul had 3 oranges.
He bought 5 more.
How many does he have
in all?

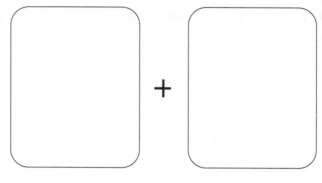

_____ oranges in all

21. Carla had 1 pencil.
Raul gave her 9 more.
How many does she have
now?

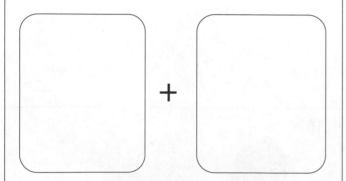

_____ pencils in all

22. Paul picked 7 beans.
Harry picked 2 beans.
How many did they pick
in all?

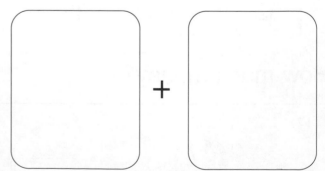

_____ beans in all

▷ Write how many.

1.

twelve ☐

2.

tens	ones

= ☐

3.

4 tens = ☐

4.

25 = ☐ tens ☐ ones

5.

hundreds	tens	ones
2	6	3

= ☐

6.

hundreds	tens	ones
4	8	1

= ☐

▷ Write each missing number.

7.

| 20 | | 22 | 23 |

8.

| 198 | | 200 | 201 |

▷ How much money?

9.
   ☐

10.
   ☐

43

▶Make a drawing to solve.

11. Gina made 3 airplanes.
John made 3 airplanes.
How many do they have
in all?

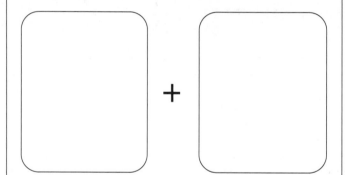

_____ airplanes in all

12. Keith made 7 cupcakes.
Sally made 2 cupcakes.
How many do they have
in all?

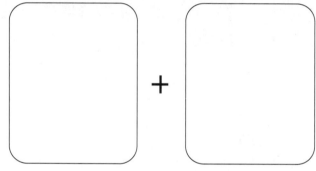

_____ cupcakes in all

13. Sharon had 2 baseballs.
She bought 4 more.
How many does she have
now?

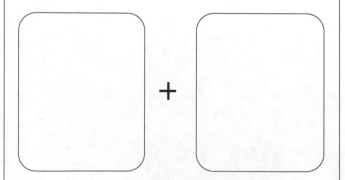

_____ baseballs in all

14. Albert won 5 blue ribbons.
He won 5 red ribbons.
How many does he have
in all?

_____ ribbons in all

3 Addition Facts Through 18

▼ ▼ ▼ ▼ ▼ ▼ ▼

Cliff cooks 9 hot dogs. Then he cooks 6 more. How many in all does he cook?

Solve

▷ Write your own problem about food.

_____

_____

_____

Adding to 11

How many  in all?

Add.

$$\begin{array}{r} 5 \\ + 6 \\ \hline 11 \end{array}$$

 in all

Guided Practice

▷ Add.

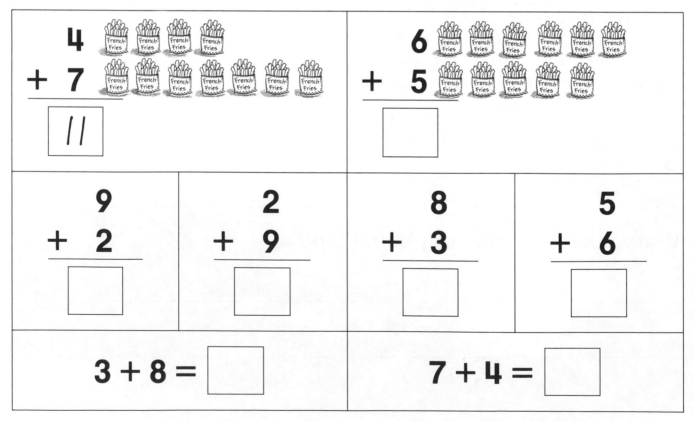

$$\begin{array}{r} 4 \\ + 7 \\ \hline 11 \end{array}$$

$$\begin{array}{r} 6 \\ + 5 \\ \hline \end{array}$$

$$\begin{array}{r} 9 \\ + 2 \\ \hline \end{array}$$

$$\begin{array}{r} 2 \\ + 9 \\ \hline \end{array}$$

$$\begin{array}{r} 8 \\ + 3 \\ \hline \end{array}$$

$$\begin{array}{r} 5 \\ + 6 \\ \hline \end{array}$$

$3 + 8 = \boxed{}$

$7 + 4 = \boxed{}$

Practice

▷ Add.

1. $\begin{array}{r} 5 \\ + 5 \\ \hline \end{array}$	2. $\begin{array}{r} 7 \\ + 4 \\ \hline \end{array}$	3. $\begin{array}{r} 3 \\ + 8 \\ \hline \end{array}$	4. $\begin{array}{r} 6 \\ + 3 \\ \hline \end{array}$
5. $\begin{array}{r} 7 \\ + 2 \\ \hline \end{array}$	6. $\begin{array}{r} 2 \\ + 9 \\ \hline \end{array}$	7. $\begin{array}{r} 8 \\ + 2 \\ \hline \end{array}$	8. $\begin{array}{r} 8 \\ + 3 \\ \hline \end{array}$

9. $9 + 2 = \boxed{}$

10. $4 + 7 = \boxed{}$

11. $8 + 1 = \boxed{}$

12. $6 + 5 = \boxed{}$

Using Math

▷ How many in all?

$$\boxed{} \\ + \boxed{} \\ \hline \boxed{}$$

 in all.

Adding to 12

How many 🎁 in all?

Add.

$$7 + 5 \over 12$$ 🎁 in all.

Guided Practice

▷ Add.

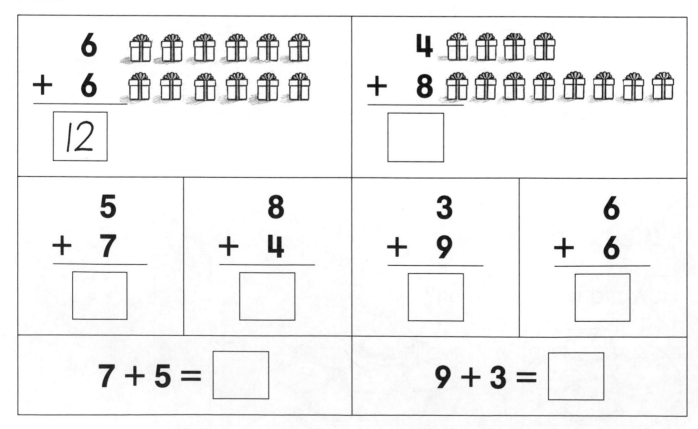

$$\begin{array}{r} 6 \\ + 6 \\ \hline \boxed{12} \end{array}$$

$$\begin{array}{r} 4 \\ + 8 \\ \hline \end{array}$$

$$\begin{array}{r} 5 \\ + 7 \\ \hline \end{array}$$

$$\begin{array}{r} 8 \\ + 4 \\ \hline \end{array}$$

$$\begin{array}{r} 3 \\ + 9 \\ \hline \end{array}$$

$$\begin{array}{r} 6 \\ + 6 \\ \hline \end{array}$$

$7 + 5 = \boxed{}$

$9 + 3 = \boxed{}$

Practice

▷Add.

1. $\begin{array}{r} 5 \\ + \ 7 \\ \hline \end{array}$ $\square$	2. $\begin{array}{r} 3 \\ + \ 9 \\ \hline \end{array}$ $\square$	3. $\begin{array}{r} 6 \\ + \ 4 \\ \hline \end{array}$ $\square$	4. $\begin{array}{r} 3 \\ + \ 8 \\ \hline \end{array}$ $\square$
5. $\begin{array}{r} 5 \\ + \ 6 \\ \hline \end{array}$ $\square$	6. $\begin{array}{r} 8 \\ + \ 2 \\ \hline \end{array}$ $\square$	7. $\begin{array}{r} 6 \\ + \ 6 \\ \hline \end{array}$ $\square$	8. $\begin{array}{r} 8 \\ + \ 4 \\ \hline \end{array}$ $\square$

9. $9 + 2 = \square$	10. $8 + 3 = \square$
11. $5 + 5 = \square$	12. $4 + 8 = \square$

Problem Solving

▷Make a drawing to solve.
Kim had 6 red apples.
She bought 3 green apples.
How many apples in all does
she have?

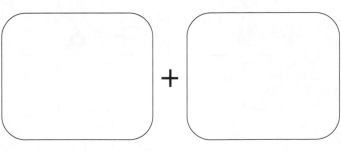

_____ apples in all

Adding to 13

How many 🔵 in all?

Add.

$$\begin{array}{r} 8 \\ + 5 \\ \hline 13 \end{array}$$ 🔵 in all.

Guided Practice

▷ Add.

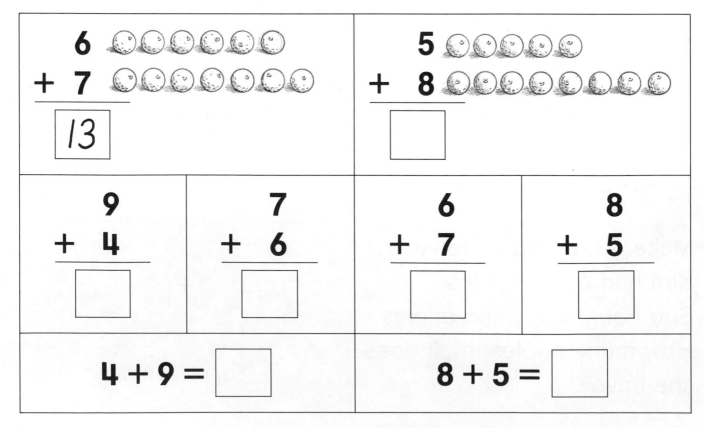

$$\begin{array}{r} 6 \\ + 7 \\ \hline \boxed{13} \end{array}$$

$$\begin{array}{r} 5 \\ + 8 \\ \hline \end{array}$$

$$\begin{array}{r} 9 \\ + 4 \\ \hline \end{array}$$

$$\begin{array}{r} 7 \\ + 6 \\ \hline \end{array}$$

$$\begin{array}{r} 6 \\ + 7 \\ \hline \end{array}$$

$$\begin{array}{r} 8 \\ + 5 \\ \hline \end{array}$$

$4 + 9 = \boxed{}$

$8 + 5 = \boxed{}$

Practice

▷ Add.

1. $\begin{array}{r} 5 \\ +\ 5 \\ \hline \end{array}$ ☐	2. $\begin{array}{r} 6 \\ +\ 7 \\ \hline \end{array}$ ☐	3. $\begin{array}{r} 7 \\ +\ 4 \\ \hline \end{array}$ ☐	4. $\begin{array}{r} 8 \\ +\ 4 \\ \hline \end{array}$ ☐
5. $\begin{array}{r} 7 \\ +\ 6 \\ \hline \end{array}$ ☐	6. $\begin{array}{r} 6 \\ +\ 6 \\ \hline \end{array}$ ☐	7. $\begin{array}{r} 5 \\ +\ 6 \\ \hline \end{array}$ ☐	8. $\begin{array}{r} 8 \\ +\ 5 \\ \hline \end{array}$ ☐

9. $5 + 8 =$ ☐	10. $7 + 5 =$ ☐
11. $9 + 4 =$ ☐	12. $9 + 2 =$ ☐

Using Math

▷ How many in all?

$$\boxed{}$$
$$+\ \boxed{}$$
$$\overline{\boxed{}}$$

 in all.

Adding to 14

<table>
<tr>
<td>How many ✦ in all?</td>
<td>Add.
7
+ 7
――――
14 ✦ in all.</td>
</tr>
</table>

Guided Practice

▷ Add.

9 + 5 14	6 + 8 ☐

7 + 7 ☐	5 + 9 ☐	9 + 5 ☐	8 + 6 ☐

9 + 5 = ☐	8 + 6 = ☐

Practice

▷ Add.

1. $\begin{array}{r} 8 \\ + 3 \\ \hline \end{array}$	2. $\begin{array}{r} 5 \\ + 9 \\ \hline \end{array}$	3. $\begin{array}{r} 7 \\ + 7 \\ \hline \end{array}$	4. $\begin{array}{r} 6 \\ + 6 \\ \hline \end{array}$
5. $\begin{array}{r} 4 \\ + 9 \\ \hline \end{array}$	6. $\begin{array}{r} 8 \\ + 4 \\ \hline \end{array}$	7. $\begin{array}{r} 8 \\ + 6 \\ \hline \end{array}$	8. $\begin{array}{r} 8 \\ + 5 \\ \hline \end{array}$

9. $5 + 7 = \square$	10. $6 + 8 = \square$
11. $5 + 5 = \square$	12. $7 + 6 = \square$

Using Math

▷ How many 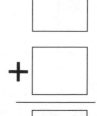 in all?

$$\begin{array}{r} \square \\ + \square \\ \hline \square \end{array}$$

 in all.

53

Adding to 15 and 16

How many 🗂 in all?	Add.
	9 + 7 ――― 16 🗂 in all.

Guided Practice

▷ Add.

| 8 🗂🗂🗂🗂🗂🗂🗂
+ 8 🗂🗂🗂🗂🗂🗂🗂🗂
――
16 | 7 🗂🗂🗂🗂🗂🗂🗂
+ 9 🗂🗂🗂🗂🗂🗂🗂🗂🗂
――
 |

8 + 7 ――	9 + 6 ――	6 + 9 ――	8 + 8 ――

7 + 8 = ▢	9 + 7 = ▢

Practice

▷ Add.

1. $\begin{array}{r} 7 \\ +\ 8 \\ \hline \end{array}$ $\square$	2. $\begin{array}{r} 3 \\ +\ 9 \\ \hline \end{array}$ $\square$	3. $\begin{array}{r} 5 \\ +\ 9 \\ \hline \end{array}$ $\square$	4. $\begin{array}{r} 7 \\ +\ 6 \\ \hline \end{array}$ $\square$
5. $\begin{array}{r} 9 \\ +\ 7 \\ \hline \end{array}$ $\square$	6. $\begin{array}{r} 6 \\ +\ 5 \\ \hline \end{array}$ $\square$	7. $\begin{array}{r} 8 \\ +\ 6 \\ \hline \end{array}$ $\square$	8. $\begin{array}{r} 5 \\ +\ 8 \\ \hline \end{array}$ $\square$

9. $6 + 9 = \square$	10. $6 + 6 = \square$
11. $8 + 7 = \square$	12. $7 + 9 = \square$

Using Math

▷ How many  in all?

$\square$ in all.

Addition Facts Through 18

How many 🌼 in all?

Add.

$$\begin{array}{r} 9 \\ + 8 \\ \hline 17 \end{array}$$ 🌼 in all.

Guided Practice

▶ Add.

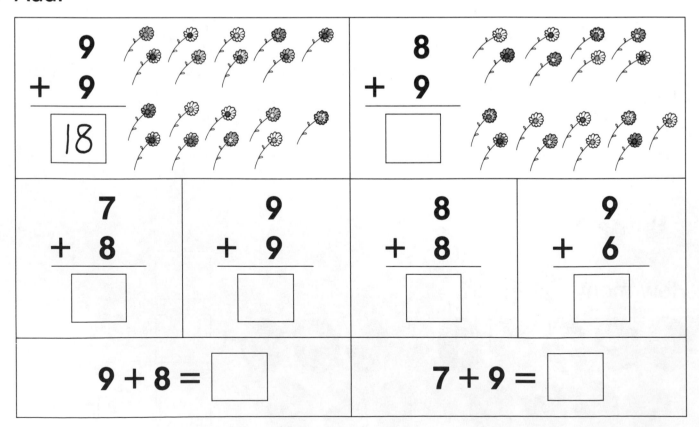

$$\begin{array}{r} 9 \\ + 9 \\ \hline 18 \end{array}$$

$$\begin{array}{r} 8 \\ + 9 \\ \hline \end{array}$$

$$\begin{array}{r} 7 \\ + 8 \\ \hline \end{array}$$

$$\begin{array}{r} 9 \\ + 9 \\ \hline \end{array}$$

$$\begin{array}{r} 8 \\ + 8 \\ \hline \end{array}$$

$$\begin{array}{r} 9 \\ + 6 \\ \hline \end{array}$$

$9 + 8 = \boxed{}$

$7 + 9 = \boxed{}$

Practice

▷Add.

1. $\begin{array}{r} 8 \\ +\ 8 \\ \hline \end{array}$	2. $\begin{array}{r} 8 \\ +\ 9 \\ \hline \end{array}$	3. $\begin{array}{r} 9 \\ +\ 6 \\ \hline \end{array}$	4. $\begin{array}{r} 9 \\ +\ 8 \\ \hline \end{array}$
5. $\begin{array}{r} 7 \\ +\ 9 \\ \hline \end{array}$	6. $\begin{array}{r} 7 \\ +\ 6 \\ \hline \end{array}$	7. $\begin{array}{r} 9 \\ +\ 9 \\ \hline \end{array}$	8. $\begin{array}{r} 8 \\ +\ 4 \\ \hline \end{array}$

9. $8 + 7 = \boxed{}$	10. $9 + 7 = \boxed{}$
11. $8 + 5 = \boxed{}$	12. $7 + 7 = \boxed{}$

Using Math

▷How many in all?

$$\boxed{}$$
$$+\ \boxed{}$$
$$\boxed{}$$ 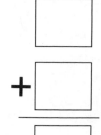 in all.

57

Quarters

quarter 25¢	quarter 25¢

 =   **=**

Guided Practice

▷ How much money?

37¢

Practice

▷How much money?

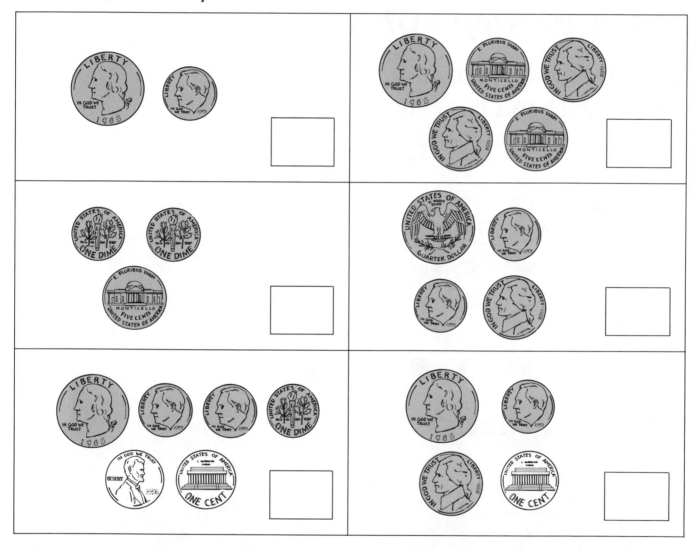

Using Math

▷Mark how much money.

Use a Pictograph

Tim helped at a bake sale.
The graph shows the cookies he sold.

Cookies Sold

	1	2	3	4	5	6	7	8
	♡	♡	♡	♡	♡	♡		
Type	☺	☺	☺	☺	☺	☺	☺	
of	▭	▭	▭					
Cookie	◉	◉	◉	◉	◉	◉	◉	◉
	❀							
	●	●	●	●	●			

Guided Practice

▶ Write how many.

♡ _6_   ❀ ____   ▭ ____

▶ Write how many. Add.

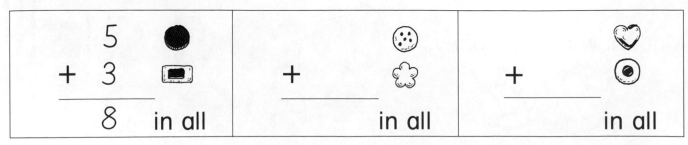

$$\begin{array}{r} 5 \\ + 3 \\ \hline 8 \end{array}$$ in all   ____ + ____ ____ in all   ____ + ____ ____ in all

60

Practice

Kay works in a store that sells shirts.
The graph shows the shirts she sold today.

Shirts Sold

	1	2	3	4	5	6	7	8
Type	👕	👕	👕	👕	👕			
of	👕	👕	👕	👕	👕	👕	👕	
Shirt	👕	👕	👕	👕				
	👕	👕	👕					
	👕	👕	👕	👕	👕	👕	👕	👕

▷ Write how many.

1.	2.	3.	4.
_____	_____	_____	_____

▷ Write how many. Add.

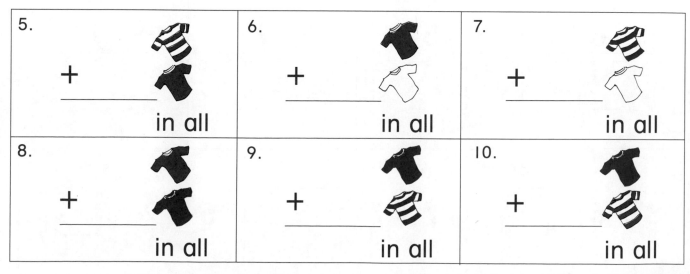

5. + _____ in all	6. + _____ in all	7. + _____ in all
8. + _____ in all	9. + _____ in all	10. + _____ in all

▸ Add.

pages 46–47

1.
$$2$$
$$+\ 9$$

2.
$$5$$
$$+\ 6$$

3.
$$3$$
$$+\ 8$$

4.
$$7$$
$$+\ 4$$

pages 48–49

5.
$$8$$
$$+\ 4$$

6.
$$6$$
$$+\ 6$$

7.
$$5$$
$$+\ 7$$

8.
$$9$$
$$+\ 3$$

pages 50–51

9.
$$7$$
$$+\ 6$$

10.
$$8$$
$$+\ 5$$

11.
$$4$$
$$+\ 9$$

12.
$$6$$
$$+\ 7$$

pages 52–53

13.
$$8 + 6 =$$

14.
$$7 + 7 =$$

15.
$$5 + 9 =$$

▷Add.

pages 54–55			
16. **8** **+ 8** ☐	17. **7** **+ 8** ☐	18. **9** **+ 7** ☐	19. **6** **+ 9** ☐
pages 56–57			
20. **8** **+ 9** ☐	21. **9** **+ 9** ☐	22. **7** **+ 9** ☐	23. **9** **+ 8** ☐

▷How much money?   pages 58–59

24.   ☐

25.   ☐

26.   ☐

Mark sold pennants at a ball game.
The graph shows the pennants he sold.

Pennants Sold

	1	2	3	4	5	6	7	8
Pennants	football	football	football	football	football	football		
	soccer	soccer	soccer	soccer				
	TEAM	TEAM	TEAM					
	baseball	baseball	baseball	baseball	baseball	baseball	baseball	baseball
	basketball	basketball	basketball	basketball	basketball	basketball	basketball	

▷ Write how many.

Add.

pages 60–61

27. baseball + basketball	28. basketball + soccer	29. football + TEAM
____ in all	____ in all	____ in all
30. soccer + football	31. TEAM + soccer	32. basketball + baseball
____ in all	____ in all	____ in all

64

▷ Add.

1. $\begin{array}{r} 7 \\ +\ 4 \\ \hline \end{array}$	2. $\begin{array}{r} 3 \\ +\ 9 \\ \hline \end{array}$	3. $\begin{array}{r} 6 \\ +\ 7 \\ \hline \end{array}$	4. $\begin{array}{r} 6 \\ +\ 5 \\ \hline \end{array}$

5. $3 + 8 = \boxed{}$

6. $8 + 4 = \boxed{}$

7. $5 + 8 = \boxed{}$

8. $\begin{array}{r} 7 \\ +\ 7 \\ \hline \end{array}$	9. $\begin{array}{r} 6 \\ +\ 9 \\ \hline \end{array}$	10. $\begin{array}{r} 9 \\ +\ 7 \\ \hline \end{array}$	11. $\begin{array}{r} 8 \\ +\ 9 \\ \hline \end{array}$

12. $9 + 9 = \boxed{}$

13. $6 + 8 = \boxed{}$

14. $8 + 8 = \boxed{}$

▷ 15. How much money?

Mr. Brown owns a farm.
He made a graph of the horses on his farm.

Horses on the Farm

	1	2	3	4	5	6	7	8

Type
of
Horse

▶Write how many.
Add.

16. +	in all	17. +	in all	18. +	in all
19. +	in all	20. +	in all	21. +	in all

Add.

pages 2–3

1.
$$
\begin{array}{r}
2 \\
+\ 1 \\
\hline
\end{array}
$$

2.
$$
\begin{array}{r}
2 \\
+\ 4 \\
\hline
\end{array}
$$

3.
$$
\begin{array}{r}
3 \\
+\ 2 \\
\hline
\end{array}
$$

4.
$$
\begin{array}{r}
2 \\
+\ 2 \\
\hline
\end{array}
$$

pages 4–5

5.
$$
\begin{array}{r}
4 \\
+\ 3 \\
\hline
\end{array}
$$

6.
$$
\begin{array}{r}
5 \\
+\ 2 \\
\hline
\end{array}
$$

7.
$$
\begin{array}{r}
2 \\
+\ 6 \\
\hline
\end{array}
$$

8.
$$
\begin{array}{r}
5 \\
+\ 3 \\
\hline
\end{array}
$$

pages 6–7

9. $2 + 8 =$ ☐

10. $6 + 3 =$ ☐

11. $7 + 2 =$ ☐

12. $5 + 5 =$ ☐

Subtract.

pages 8–9

13.
$$
\begin{array}{r}
3 \\
-\ 1 \\
\hline
\end{array}
$$

14.
$$
\begin{array}{r}
6 \\
-\ 2 \\
\hline
\end{array}
$$

15.
$$
\begin{array}{r}
4 \\
-\ 3 \\
\hline
\end{array}
$$

16.
$$
\begin{array}{r}
5 \\
-\ 0 \\
\hline
\end{array}
$$

▷Subtract.

pages 10–11 17. $\begin{array}{r} 8 \\ -\ 5 \\ \hline \end{array}$ $\square$	18. $\begin{array}{r} 7 \\ -\ 3 \\ \hline \end{array}$ $\square$	19. $\begin{array}{r} 8 \\ -\ 4 \\ \hline \end{array}$ $\square$	20. $\begin{array}{r} 7 \\ -\ 1 \\ \hline \end{array}$ $\square$

pages 12–13

21. $10 - 3 = \square$ 22. $9 - 6 = \square$

23. $9 - 7 = \square$ 24. $10 - 9 = \square$

25. $10 - 6 = \square$ 26. $9 - 1 = \square$

▷How much money?

pages 14–15

27. $\square$

28. $\square$

▷**Write how many.** pages 16–17

29.	30.	31.
_____	_____	_____
32.	33.	34.
_____	_____	_____

▷**Write how many.**
Add.

35.	36.	37.
+ _____	+ _____	+ _____
in all	in all	in all

Write how many.

pages 24–25

1. 	2. 	3. 
thirteen ☐	fourteen ☐	sixteen ☐

pages 26–27

4.

tens	ones

= ☐

5.

tens	ones

= ☐

6.

tens	ones

= ☐

7.

tens	ones

= ☐

pages 28–29

8.	9.	10.
3 tens = ☐	6 tens = ☐	9 tens = ☐

Write how many. pages 30–31

11.
52 = ☐ tens ☐ ones

12.
89 = ☐ tens ☐ ones

pages 32–33

13.
hundreds	tens	ones
2	6	3

= ☐

14.
hundreds	tens	ones
8	4	7

= ☐

15.
hundreds	tens	ones
1	1	1

= ☐

16.
hundreds	tens	ones
9	2	0

= ☐

Write each missing number. pages 34–35

17.
| 42 | | 44 | 45 |

18.
| 901 | 902 | 903 | |

How much money? pages 36–37

19.
   ☐

20.
   ☐

▶**Make a drawing to solve.** pages 38–39

21. Ann had 5 flowers.
She picked 4 more.
How many does she have
in all?

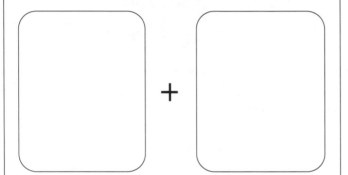

_____ flowers in all

22. Ricco has 2 big rabbits
and 6 baby rabbits.
How many does he have
in all?

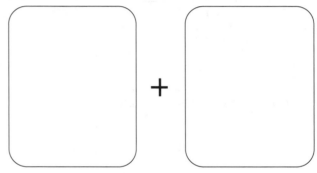

_____ rabbits in all

23. Abe had 3 pieces of chalk.
Lucy gave him 7 more.
How many does he have
now?

_____ pieces of chalk

24. Mei had 8 crayons.
She found 1 more
crayon. How many does
she have now?

_____ crayons in all

▷ Add.

pages 46–51

1.
$$\begin{array}{r} 8 \\ + 3 \\ \hline \end{array}$$

2.
$$\begin{array}{r} 6 \\ + 6 \\ \hline \end{array}$$

3.
$$\begin{array}{r} 7 \\ + 4 \\ \hline \end{array}$$

4.
$$\begin{array}{r} 5 \\ + 8 \\ \hline \end{array}$$

5. $3 + 9 =$ ☐

6. $7 + 6 =$ ☐

7. $9 + 4 =$ ☐

pages 52–57

8.
$$\begin{array}{r} 9 \\ + 5 \\ \hline \end{array}$$

9.
$$\begin{array}{r} 8 \\ + 6 \\ \hline \end{array}$$

10.
$$\begin{array}{r} 8 \\ + 7 \\ \hline \end{array}$$

11.
$$\begin{array}{r} 9 \\ + 6 \\ \hline \end{array}$$

12. $9 + 9 =$ ☐

13. $8 + 9 =$ ☐

14. $9 + 7 =$ ☐

▷ How much money? pages 58–59

15.   ☐

Leah sells cars.

She made a graph to show the cars she sold last month.

Cars Sold

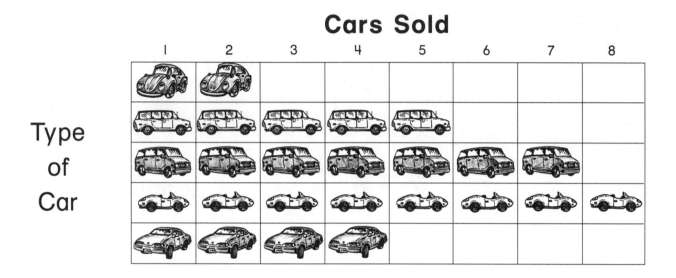

Type
of
Car

▷Write how many.

Add.

pages 60–61

| 16.
+ _____ in all | 17.
+ _____ in all | 18.
+ _____ in all |
| 19.
+ _____ in all | 20.
+ _____ in all | 21.
+ _____ in all |

Subtraction Facts Through 18

Pug had 7 puppies. The boys take away 2 of them. How many puppies are left?

Solve

▶Write your own problem about pets.

Subtracting from 11

How many 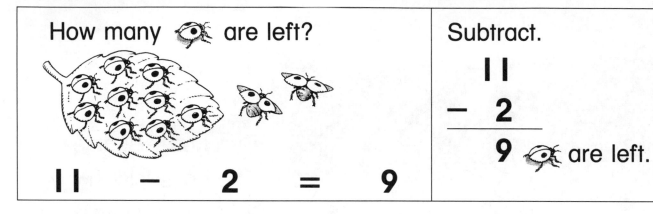 are left?

11 – 2 = 9

Subtract.

$$11$$
$$-\ 2$$
$$9$$ are left.

Guided Practice

▷ Subtract.

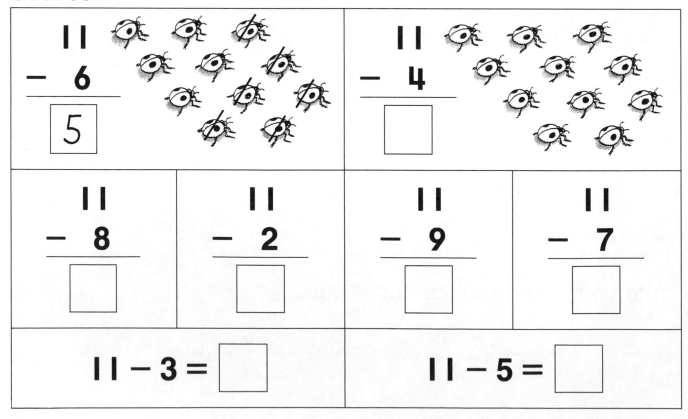

$$11 - 6 = \boxed{5}$$

$$11 - 4 = \boxed{}$$

$$11 - 8 = \boxed{}$$

$$11 - 2 = \boxed{}$$

$$11 - 9 = \boxed{}$$

$$11 - 7 = \boxed{}$$

$$11 - 3 = \boxed{}$$

$$11 - 5 = \boxed{}$$

Practice

▶Subtract.

1. $\begin{array}{r} 11 \\ -\ 2 \\ \hline \square \end{array}$	2. $\begin{array}{r} 10 \\ -\ 4 \\ \hline \square \end{array}$	3. $\begin{array}{r} 9 \\ -\ 5 \\ \hline \square \end{array}$	4. $\begin{array}{r} 11 \\ -\ 4 \\ \hline \square \end{array}$
5. $\begin{array}{r} 9 \\ -\ 6 \\ \hline \square \end{array}$	6. $\begin{array}{r} 11 \\ -\ 9 \\ \hline \square \end{array}$	7. $\begin{array}{r} 11 \\ -\ 7 \\ \hline \square \end{array}$	8. $\begin{array}{r} 11 \\ -\ 3 \\ \hline \square \end{array}$

9. $11 - 8 = \square$	10. $11 - 6 = \square$
11. $10 - 7 = \square$	12. $11 - 5 = \square$

Using Math

▶There are 11 ladybugs.

7 ladybugs fly away.

How many are left?

$$\begin{array}{r} \square \\ -\ \square \\ \hline \square \end{array}$$

77

Subtracting from 12

How many 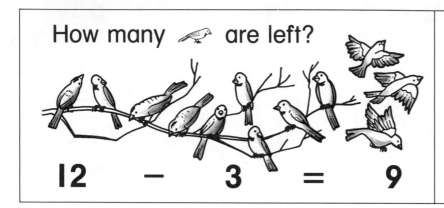 are left?

12   −   3   =   9

Subtract.

$$\begin{array}{r} 12 \\ -\ 3 \\ \hline 9 \end{array}$$ are left.

Guided Practice

▷ Subtract.

$$\begin{array}{r} 12 \\ -\ 7 \\ \hline \boxed{5} \end{array}$$

$$\begin{array}{r} 12 \\ -\ 4 \\ \hline \end{array}$$

$$\begin{array}{r} 12 \\ -\ 6 \\ \hline \end{array}$$

$$\begin{array}{r} 12 \\ -\ 3 \\ \hline \end{array}$$

$$\begin{array}{r} 12 \\ -\ 9 \\ \hline \end{array}$$

$$\begin{array}{r} 12 \\ -\ 7 \\ \hline \end{array}$$

12 − 5 = ☐

12 − 8 = ☐

Practice

Subtract.

1.   12
   − 3
☐
	2. 11
	   − 6
	☐

1.   12
   − 3
☐

2.   11
   − 6
☐

3.   12
   − 8
☐

4.   12
   − 6
☐

5.   12
   − 4
☐

6.   11
   − 2
☐

7.   12
   − 7
☐

8.   11
   − 5
☐

9. $12 - 9 = $ ☐

10. $11 - 3 = $ ☐

11. $11 - 6 = $ ☐

12. $12 - 5 = $ ☐

Using Math

There are 12 pigs.

4 pigs go play in the mud.

How many are left?

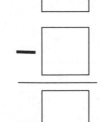

79

Subtracting from 13

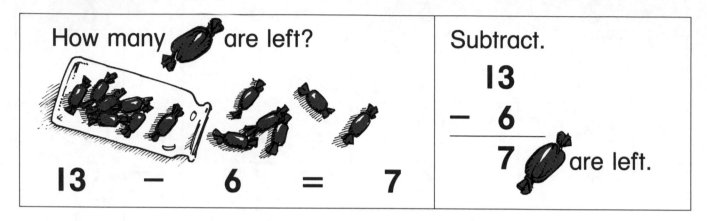

How many 🍬 are left?

13   –   6   =   7

Subtract.

$$\begin{array}{r} 13 \\ -\ 6 \\ \hline 7 \end{array}$$ 🍬 are left.

Guided Practice

▷ Subtract.

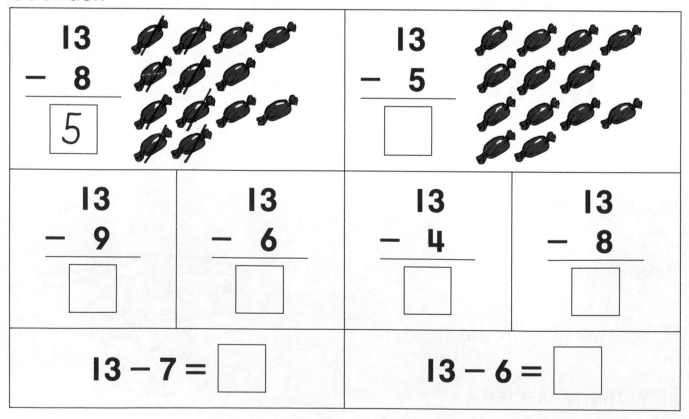

$$\begin{array}{r} 13 \\ -\ 8 \\ \hline \boxed{5} \end{array}$$

$$\begin{array}{r} 13 \\ -\ 5 \\ \hline \end{array}$$

$$\begin{array}{r} 13 \\ -\ 9 \\ \hline \end{array}$$

$$\begin{array}{r} 13 \\ -\ 6 \\ \hline \end{array}$$

$$\begin{array}{r} 13 \\ -\ 4 \\ \hline \end{array}$$

$$\begin{array}{r} 13 \\ -\ 8 \\ \hline \end{array}$$

13 – 7 = ☐

13 – 6 = ☐

Practice

▷Subtract.

1. 13 − 5 □	2. 12 − 5 □	3. 13 − 6 □	4. 13 − 9 □
5. 9 − 6 □	6. 13 − 8 □	7. 10 − 1 □	8. 13 − 4 □

9. 12 − 6 = □

10. 11 − 5 = □

11. 13 − 7 = □

12. 11 − 4 = □

Using Math

▷There are 13 pieces of candy.

5 pieces are unwrapped.

How many are left?

□
− □
□

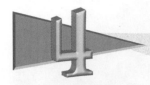

Subtracting from 14

How many 🌼 are left?

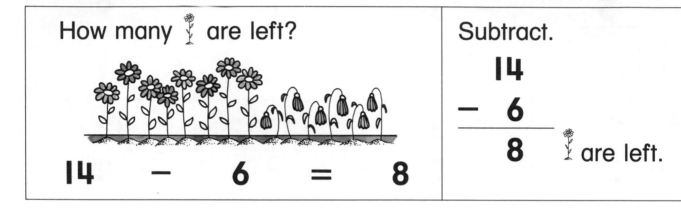

14   −   6   =   8

Subtract.

$$\begin{array}{r} 14 \\ -\ 6 \\ \hline 8 \end{array}$$ 🌼 are left.

Guided Practice

▷ Subtract.

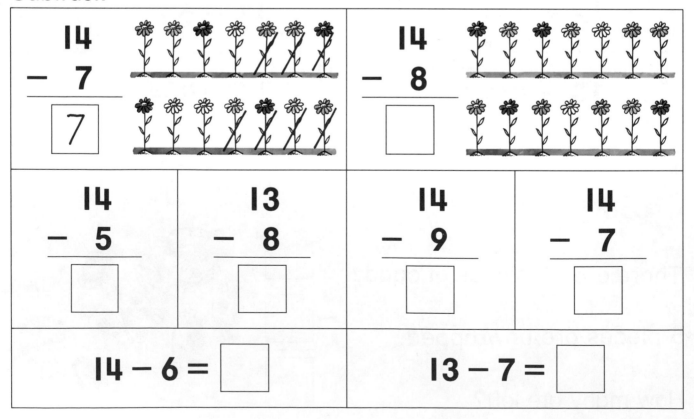

$$\begin{array}{r} 14 \\ -\ 7 \\ \hline \boxed{7} \end{array}$$

$$\begin{array}{r} 14 \\ -\ 8 \\ \hline \boxed{} \end{array}$$

$$\begin{array}{r} 14 \\ -\ 5 \\ \hline \boxed{} \end{array}$$

$$\begin{array}{r} 13 \\ -\ 8 \\ \hline \boxed{} \end{array}$$

$$\begin{array}{r} 14 \\ -\ 9 \\ \hline \boxed{} \end{array}$$

$$\begin{array}{r} 14 \\ -\ 7 \\ \hline \boxed{} \end{array}$$

14 − 6 = ☐

13 − 7 = ☐

Practice

▷Subtract.

1. $14 - 9 = \square$	2. $13 - 4 = \square$	3. $12 - 6 = \square$	4. $14 - 5 = \square$
5. $14 - 8 = \square$	6. $12 - 5 = \square$	7. $13 - 8 = \square$	8. $14 - 9 = \square$

9. $14 - 6 = \square$ 10. $13 - 9 = \square$

11. $14 - 7 = \square$ 12. $11 - 3 = \square$

Problem Solving

▷Write how many.
Add.

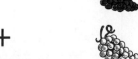

$$+ \underline{\hspace{3cm}}$$

in all

Grapes

	Type of Grape	1	2	3	4

Subtracting from 15 and 16

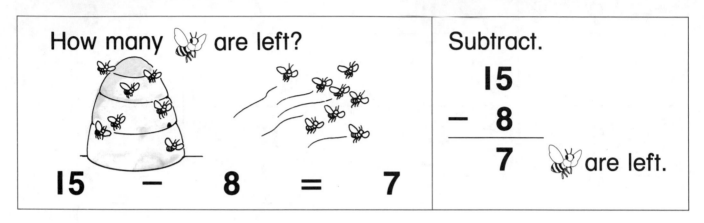

How many 🐝 are left?

15 − 8 = 7

Subtract.

15
− 8
——
7 🐝 are left.

Guided Practice

▷ Subtract.

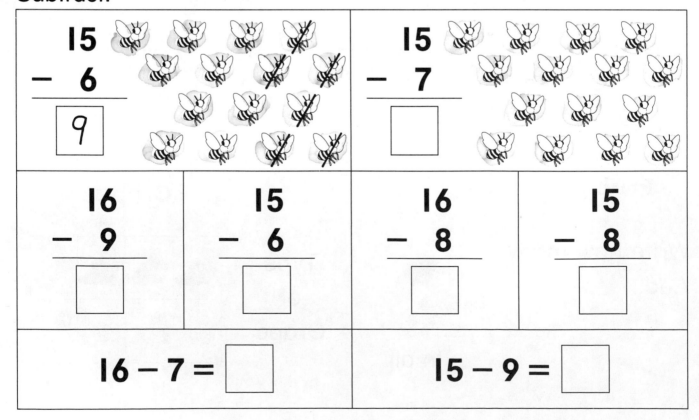

15 − 6 —— 9	15 − 7 —— ☐

16 − 9 —— ☐	15 − 6 —— ☐	16 − 8 —— ☐	15 − 8 —— ☐

16 − 7 = ☐	15 − 9 = ☐

Practice

▷Subtract.

1.   16
  − 9
☐
	2. 15
	  − 7
	☐
		3. 16
		  − 8
		☐
			4. 15
			  − 6
			☐

5.   15
  − 8
☐
	6. 16
	  − 7
	☐
		7. 15
		  − 9
		☐
			8. 14
			  − 7
			☐

9. 15 − 7 = ☐	10. 13 − 9 = ☐
11. 14 − 8 = ☐	12. 15 − 6 = ☐

Using Math

▷There are 15 bees.

9 bees fly away.

How many are left?

☐
− ☐
☐

Subtraction Facts Through 18

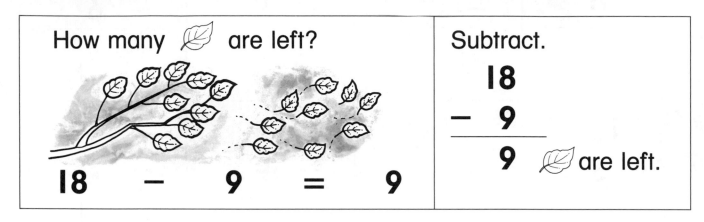

How many 🍃 are left?

18 – 9 = 9

Subtract.

18
– 9
———
9 🍃 are left.

Guided Practice

▷ Subtract.

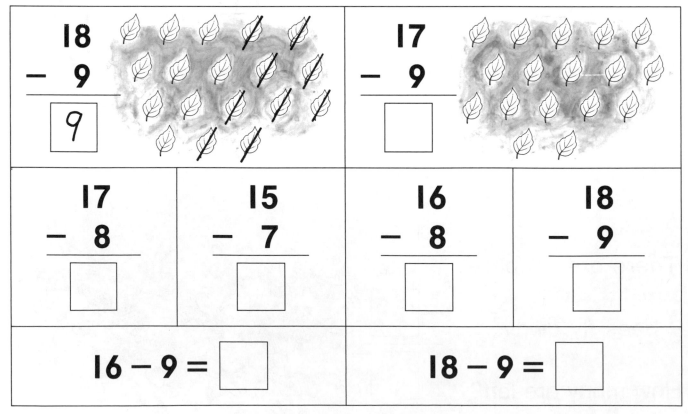

18
– 9
———
9

17
– 9
———
☐

17
– 8
———
☐

15
– 7
———
☐

16
– 8
———
☐

18
– 9
———
☐

16 – 9 = ☐

18 – 9 = ☐

Practice

▶Subtract.

1. $\begin{array}{r} 14 \\ -\ 8 \\ \hline \square \end{array}$	2. $\begin{array}{r} 18 \\ -\ 9 \\ \hline \square \end{array}$	3. $\begin{array}{r} 17 \\ -\ 9 \\ \hline \square \end{array}$	4. $\begin{array}{r} 17 \\ -\ 8 \\ \hline \square \end{array}$
5. $\begin{array}{r} 16 \\ -\ 9 \\ \hline \square \end{array}$	6. $\begin{array}{r} 16 \\ -\ 7 \\ \hline \square \end{array}$	7. $\begin{array}{r} 15 \\ -\ 6 \\ \hline \square \end{array}$	8. $\begin{array}{r} 16 \\ -\ 8 \\ \hline \square \end{array}$

9. $15 - 7 = \square$

10. $14 - 7 = \square$

11. $14 - 5 = \square$

12. $15 - 9 = \square$

Using Math

▶There are 17 butterflies.

8 butterflies fly away.

How many are left?

Half Dollar

half dollar 50¢ 	half dollar 50¢ 

 =    =

Guided Practice

▷How much money?

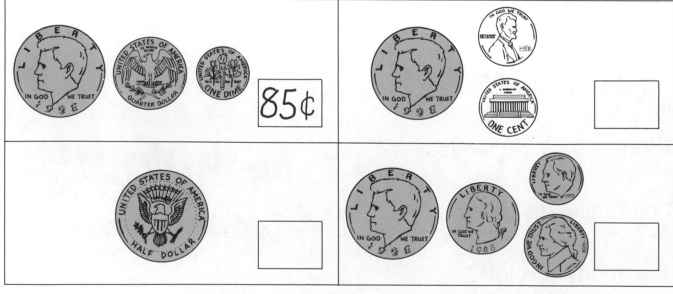

85¢

88

Practice

▷How much money?

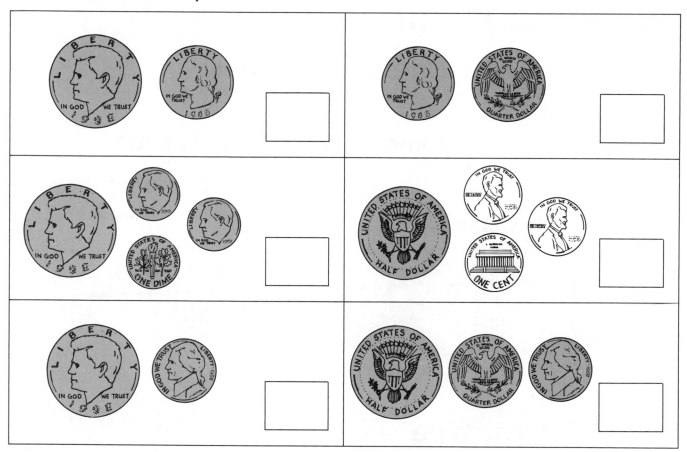

Using Math

▷Mark how much money.

Problem Solving

Use a Bar Graph

Zack made a graph to show the students
in his art class each day.

Number of Students in Art

	1	2	3	4	5	6	7	8
Monday								
Tuesday								
Wednesday								
Thursday								
Friday								

Guided Practice

▷ Write how many.

Thursday __6__	Monday _____	Wednesday _____

▷ Write how many. Add.

$\begin{array}{r} 3 \\ +\ 6 \\ \hline 9 \end{array}$ Tuesday Thursday in all	$\begin{array}{r} \\ +\ \\ \hline \end{array}$ Monday Friday in all	$\begin{array}{r} \\ +\ \\ \hline \end{array}$ Wednesday Tuesday in all

Practice

Abe made a graph to show the dogs his friends have.

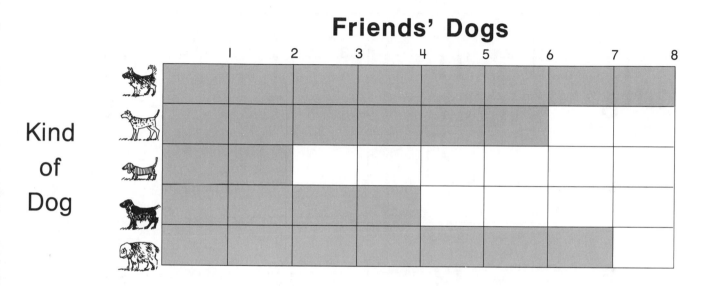

Friends' Dogs

Kind of Dog

▷ Write how many.

1.	2.	3.	4.

▷ Write how many. Add.

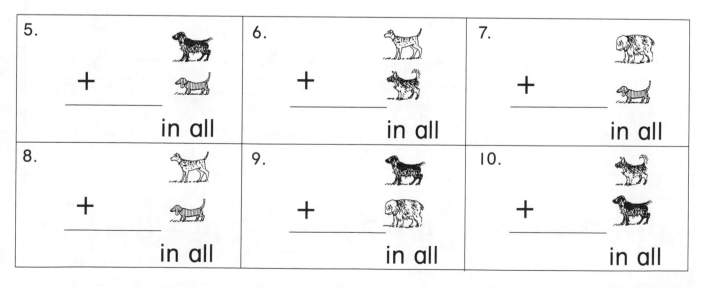

5. + _____ in all	6. + _____ in all	7. + _____ in all
8. + _____ in all	9. + _____ in all	10. + _____ in all

▷ Subtract.

pages 76–77			
1. $\begin{array}{r} 11 \\ -\ 6 \\ \hline \square \end{array}$	2. $\begin{array}{r} 11 \\ -\ 2 \\ \hline \square \end{array}$	3. $\begin{array}{r} 11 \\ -\ 7 \\ \hline \square \end{array}$	4. $\begin{array}{r} 11 \\ -\ 8 \\ \hline \square \end{array}$

pages 78–79			
5. $\begin{array}{r} 12 \\ -\ 8 \\ \hline \square \end{array}$	6. $\begin{array}{r} 12 \\ -\ 6 \\ \hline \square \end{array}$	7. $\begin{array}{r} 12 \\ -\ 3 \\ \hline \square \end{array}$	8. $\begin{array}{r} 12 \\ -\ 7 \\ \hline \square \end{array}$

pages 80–81			
9. $\begin{array}{r} 13 \\ -\ 7 \\ \hline \square \end{array}$	10. $\begin{array}{r} 13 \\ -\ 4 \\ \hline \square \end{array}$	11. $\begin{array}{r} 13 \\ -\ 8 \\ \hline \square \end{array}$	12. $\begin{array}{r} 13 \\ -\ 5 \\ \hline \square \end{array}$

pages 82–83		
13. $14 - 9 = \square$	14. $14 - 7 = \square$	15. $14 - 8 = \square$

Subtract.

pages 84–85

16.
$$15$$
$$- \ 8$$

17.
$$16$$
$$- \ 7$$

18.
$$15$$
$$- \ 6$$

19.
$$16$$
$$- \ 9$$

pages 86–87

20. $18 - 9 =$

21. $17 - 8 =$

22. $16 - 8 =$

▷ How much money? pages 88–89

23.

24.

25.

Rita asked the students in her class to name their favorite type of shoes. The graph shows how many students like each kind of shoe.

Favorite Shoes

▷ Write how many.
Add.
pages 90–91

26. 	27.	28.
+ ___ in all	+ ___ in all	+ ___ in all
29.	30.	31.
+ ___ in all	+ ___ in all	+ ___ in all

94

 **Test**

►Subtract.

1. 11 − 2 ☐	2. 12 − 3 ☐	3. 13 − 9 ☐	4. 13 − 6 ☐
5. 11 − 8 = ☐	6. 13 − 8 = ☐	7. 12 − 7 = ☐	
8. 14 − 8 ☐	9. 15 − 6 ☐	10. 16 − 9 ☐	11. 17 − 9 ☐
12. 18 − 9 = ☐	13. 16 − 8 = ☐	14. 17 − 8 = ☐	

►How much money?

15.    ☐

Ms. Clark asked her class
what type sports they
like. She made a graph
to show the numbers of
students who like
each sport.

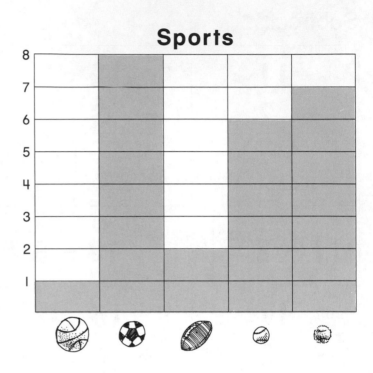

Sports

▷ Write how many.
Add.

16.
 + _____
           in all
	17.
	 + _____
	           in all
		18.
		 + _____
		           in all

19.
 + _____
           in all
	20.
	 + _____
	           in all
		21.
		 + _____
		           in all

Adding and Subtracting 2-Digit Numbers

Rita sells 24 tickets to the fair. Diaz sells 15 tickets. How many do they sell in all?

Solve

▷ Write your own problem about going to a fair.

Adding Ones and Tens

How many in all?

24 + 5

24
+ 5
———

Add.

Step 1		Add the ones.

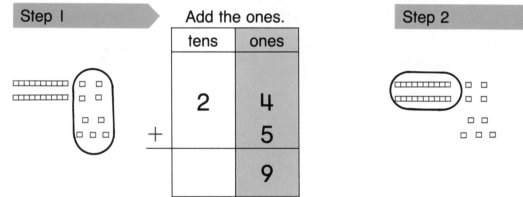

tens	ones
2	4
+	5
	9

Step 2		Add the tens.

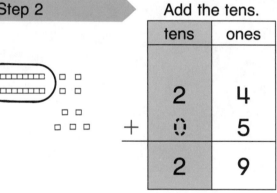

tens	ones
2	4
+ 0	5
2	9

Guided Practice

▷ Add.

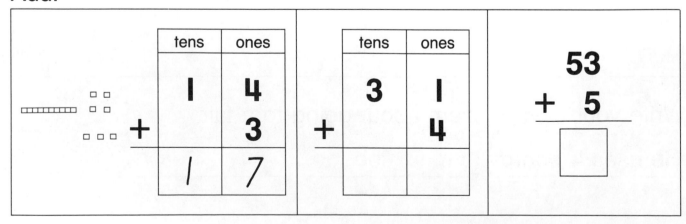

tens	ones
1	4
+	3
1	7

tens	ones
3	1
+	4

53
+ 5
———

Practice

▷ Add.

1. $\begin{array}{r} 62 \\ +\ 2 \\ \hline \end{array}$ ☐	2. $\begin{array}{r} 80 \\ +\ 1 \\ \hline \end{array}$ ☐	3. $\begin{array}{r} 21 \\ +\ 5 \\ \hline \end{array}$ ☐	4. $\begin{array}{r} 35 \\ +\ 4 \\ \hline \end{array}$ ☐
5. $\begin{array}{r} 43 \\ +\ 5 \\ \hline \end{array}$ ☐	6. $\begin{array}{r} 73 \\ +\ 3 \\ \hline \end{array}$ ☐	7. $\begin{array}{r} 52 \\ +\ 1 \\ \hline \end{array}$ ☐	8. $\begin{array}{r} 95 \\ +\ 2 \\ \hline \end{array}$ ☐
9. $\begin{array}{r} 84 \\ +\ 1 \\ \hline \end{array}$ ☐	10. $\begin{array}{r} 63 \\ +\ 4 \\ \hline \end{array}$ ☐	11. $\begin{array}{r} 36 \\ +\ 2 \\ \hline \end{array}$ ☐	12. $\begin{array}{r} 70 \\ +\ 4 \\ \hline \end{array}$ ☐

Using Math

▷ Carlos made a car.
He used 10 boards to make the bottom.
He used 4 boards to make the top.
How many boards did he use in all?

☐
+ ☐
―――
☐

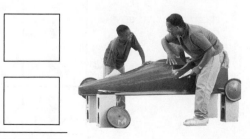

He used ____ boards in all.

Adding Two 2-Digit Numbers

How many in all?		Add.
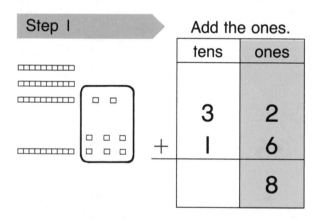 32 + 16		32 + 16

Step 1 ▶ Add the ones.

tens	ones
3	2
+ 1	6
	8

Step 2 ▶ Add the tens.

tens	ones
3	2
+ 1	6
4	8

Guided Practice

▷ Add.

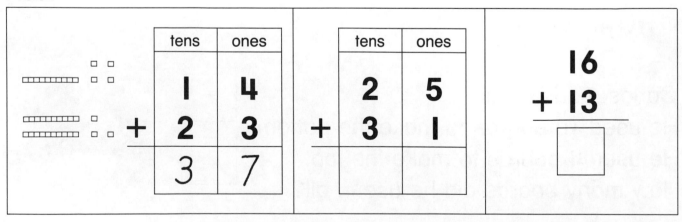

tens	ones
1	4
+ 2	3
3	7

tens	ones
2	5
+ 3	1

16
+ 13

☐

100

Practice

▷ Add.

1. $\begin{array}{r} 17 \\ +31 \\ \hline \square \end{array}$	2. $\begin{array}{r} 43 \\ +26 \\ \hline \square \end{array}$	3. $\begin{array}{r} 34 \\ +51 \\ \hline \square \end{array}$	4. $\begin{array}{r} 62 \\ +10 \\ \hline \square \end{array}$
5. $\begin{array}{r} 43 \\ +52 \\ \hline \square \end{array}$	6. $\begin{array}{r} 26 \\ +12 \\ \hline \square \end{array}$	7. $\begin{array}{r} 20 \\ +73 \\ \hline \square \end{array}$	8. $\begin{array}{r} 13 \\ +54 \\ \hline \square \end{array}$
9. $\begin{array}{r} 27 \\ +62 \\ \hline \square \end{array}$	10. $\begin{array}{r} 30 \\ +30 \\ \hline \square \end{array}$	11. $\begin{array}{r} 52 \\ +23 \\ \hline \square \end{array}$	12. $\begin{array}{r} 35 \\ +13 \\ \hline \square \end{array}$

Using Math

▷ Ms. Ford's class was in the parade.
13 children rode on the fire truck.
14 children rode on a float.
How many children were in the parade?

$\begin{array}{r} \square \\ + \quad \square \\ \hline \square \end{array}$

_____ children were in the parade.

Addition with Regrouping

Step 1

Add the ones.

tens	ones
[1]	
3	8
+ 1	4
	2

8 ones + 4 ones = 12 ones
Regroup 12 ones as
1 ten 2 ones.
Write the 2 in the
ones' place.
Write the 1 in the tens' box.

Step 2

Add the tens.

tens	ones
[1]	
3	8
+ 1	4
5	2

Guided Practice

▷ Add.

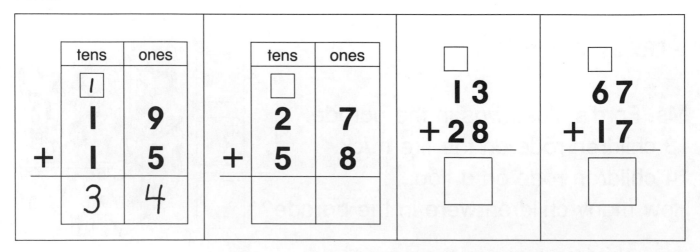

Practice

▷ Add.

1. ☐ 54 +19 ☐	2. ☐ 48 +46 ☐	3. ☐ 37 +24 ☐	4. ☐ 18 +38 ☐	5. ☐ 44 +38 ☐
6. ☐ 17 +47 ☐	7. ☐ 63 +27 ☐	8. ☐ 29 +16 ☐	9. ☐ 28 +47 ☐	10. ☐ 27 +25 ☐

Problem Solving

▷ Write how many.
Add.

+ _____

in all

This graph shows the
pizzas eaten at a party.

Type of Pizza

	1	2	3	4	5	6
Pepperoni						
Sausage						

Subtracting Ones and Tens

How many are left? | Subtract.

18   —   6

$$\begin{array}{r} 18 \\ -\ \ 6 \\ \hline \end{array}$$

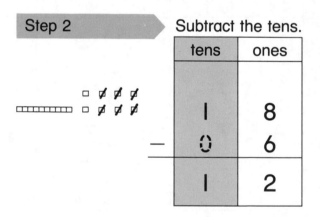

Step 1 → Subtract the ones.

tens	ones
1	8
−	6
	2

Step 2 → Subtract the tens.

tens	ones
1	8
− 0	6
1	2

Guided Practice

▷Subtract.

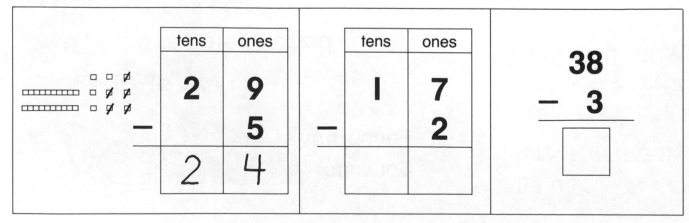

tens	ones
2	9
−	5
2	4

tens	ones
1	7
−	2

$$\begin{array}{r} 38 \\ -\ \ 3 \\ \hline \ \ \ \ \end{array}$$

Practice

▶Subtract.

1. $\begin{array}{r} 37 \\ -\ 3 \\ \hline \square \end{array}$	2. $\begin{array}{r} 64 \\ -\ 2 \\ \hline \square \end{array}$	3. $\begin{array}{r} 59 \\ -\ 6 \\ \hline \square \end{array}$	4. $\begin{array}{r} 85 \\ -\ 4 \\ \hline \square \end{array}$
5. $\begin{array}{r} 42 \\ -\ 2 \\ \hline \square \end{array}$	6. $\begin{array}{r} 98 \\ -\ 4 \\ \hline \square \end{array}$	7. $\begin{array}{r} 68 \\ -\ 2 \\ \hline \square \end{array}$	8. $\begin{array}{r} 75 \\ -\ 3 \\ \hline \square \end{array}$
9. $\begin{array}{r} 28 \\ -\ 5 \\ \hline \square \end{array}$	10. $\begin{array}{r} 86 \\ -\ 2 \\ \hline \square \end{array}$	11. $\begin{array}{r} 76 \\ -\ 1 \\ \hline \square \end{array}$	12. $\begin{array}{r} 94 \\ -\ 3 \\ \hline \square \end{array}$

Using Math

▶There are 15 cars at the track.
2 cars drive away.
How many cars are left?

_____ cars are left.

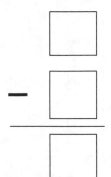

105

Subtracting Two 2-Digit Numbers

How many are left?	Subtract.

How many are left?

34   −   12

Subtract.

```
   34
 − 12
```

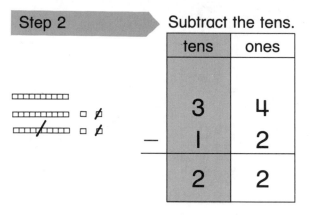

Step 1 ➤ Subtract the ones.

tens	ones
3	4
1	2
	2

Step 2 ➤ Subtract the tens.

tens	ones
3	4
1	2
2	2

Guided Practice

▷ Subtract.

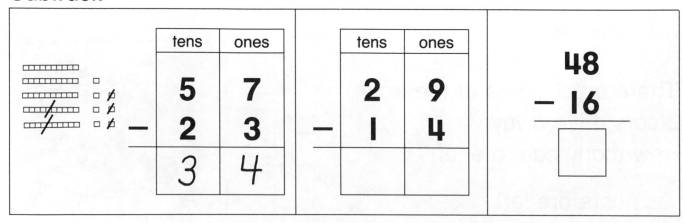

tens	ones
5	7
2	3
3	4

tens	ones
2	9
1	4

```
   48
 − 16
 ____
 [  ]
```

106

Practice

▷ Subtract.

1. $\begin{array}{r} 46 \\ -21 \\ \hline \end{array}$	2. $\begin{array}{r} 78 \\ -35 \\ \hline \end{array}$	3. $\begin{array}{r} 97 \\ -25 \\ \hline \end{array}$	4. $\begin{array}{r} 86 \\ -72 \\ \hline \end{array}$
5. $\begin{array}{r} 52 \\ -32 \\ \hline \end{array}$	6. $\begin{array}{r} 87 \\ -31 \\ \hline \end{array}$	7. $\begin{array}{r} 65 \\ -34 \\ \hline \end{array}$	8. $\begin{array}{r} 89 \\ -21 \\ \hline \end{array}$
9. $\begin{array}{r} 49 \\ -34 \\ \hline \end{array}$	10. $\begin{array}{r} 87 \\ -40 \\ \hline \end{array}$	11. $\begin{array}{r} 97 \\ -62 \\ \hline \end{array}$	12. $\begin{array}{r} 36 \\ -15 \\ \hline \end{array}$

Using Math

▷ Kate has 97 tickets to sell.
She sold 72 tickets.
How many does she have left?

_____ tickets are left?

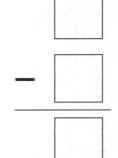

Subtraction with Regrouping

Can you subtract the ones? No.

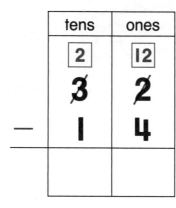

tens	ones
2	12
~~3~~	~~2~~
− 1	4

Regroup.

3 tens 2 ones = 2 tens 12 ones

Step 2

Subtract the ones.

tens	ones
2	12
~~3~~	~~2~~
− 1	4
	8

Step 3

Subtract the tens.

tens	ones
2	12
~~3~~	~~2~~
− 1	4
1	8

Guided Practice

▷Subtract.

tens	ones
1	15
2̶	5̶
− 1	9
	6

tens	ones
☐	☐
4	3
− 1	8

tens	ones
☐	☐
5	1
− 3	2

Practice

▷Subtract.

1.
```
  ☐ ☐
  3 6
− 2 8
─────
  ☐
```

2.
```
  ☐ ☐
  5 0
− 2 7
─────
  ☐
```

3.
```
  ☐ ☐
  6 2
− 4 3
─────
  ☐
```

4.
```
  ☐ ☐
  7 1
− 2 5
─────
  ☐
```

5.
```
  ☐ ☐
  9 0
− 5 5
─────
  ☐
```

6.
```
  ☐ ☐
  7 3
− 1 6
─────
  ☐
```

7.
```
  ☐ ☐
  4 6
− 3 7
─────
  ☐
```

8.
```
  ☐ ☐
  6 0
− 2 2
─────
  ☐
```

9.
```
  ☐ ☐
  8 5
− 3 8
─────
  ☐
```

10.
```
  ☐ ☐
  9 1
− 2 8
─────
  ☐
```

Dollar

one dollar
$1.00

	dollar	cents
100¢ =	**$1** .	**00**

Guided Practice

▷ How much money?

dollar	cents
$ 1 .	36

dollar	cents
.	

Practice

▷How much money?

dollar	cents
$	•

dollar	cents
$	•

dollars	cents
$	•

Using Math

▷Mark how much money.

111

Choose an Operation

Susan had 20 stamps in a book. She got 10 more stamps. How many stamps does she have in all?

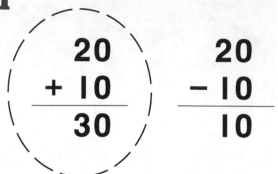

$$\begin{array}{r} 20 \\ +\ 10 \\ \hline 30 \end{array} \qquad \begin{array}{r} 20 \\ -\ 10 \\ \hline 10 \end{array}$$

Susan added because she put all the stamps together. That means she now has more.

> Add to put groups together.
> Subtract to take some away.

Guided Practice

▷ Ring the correct problem.
Ed had 46 marbles.
He gave 32 marbles away.
How many does he have left?

$$\begin{array}{r} 46 \\ +\ 32 \\ \hline 78 \end{array} \qquad \begin{array}{r} 46 \\ -\ 32 \\ \hline 14 \end{array}$$

Ed subtracted because he gave some marbles away. That means he now has less.

Practice

▷Ring the correct problem.

1.	Ken made 36 cupcakes. He gave 13 cupcakes away. How many does he have left?	$\begin{array}{r} 36 \\ +\ 13 \\ \hline 49 \end{array}$	$\begin{array}{r} 36 \\ -\ 13 \\ \hline 23 \end{array}$
2.	Ann has 20 large puzzles. She has 20 small puzzles. How many does she have in all?	$\begin{array}{r} 20 \\ +\ 20 \\ \hline 40 \end{array}$	$\begin{array}{r} 20 \\ -\ 20 \\ \hline 0 \end{array}$
3.	Tammy had 64 baseball cards. She got 10 more baseball cards. How many does she have in all?	$\begin{array}{r} 64 \\ +\ 10 \\ \hline 74 \end{array}$	$\begin{array}{r} 64 \\ -\ 10 \\ \hline 54 \end{array}$
4.	Kyle made 26 cookies. He gave 22 cookies away to friends. How many does he have left?	$\begin{array}{r} 26 \\ +\ 22 \\ \hline 48 \end{array}$	$\begin{array}{r} 26 \\ -\ 22 \\ \hline 4 \end{array}$
5.	Emil won 46 first place ribbons. He won 31 second place ribbons. How many does he have in all?	$\begin{array}{r} 46 \\ +\ 31 \\ \hline 77 \end{array}$	$\begin{array}{r} 46 \\ -\ 31 \\ \hline 15 \end{array}$

▷ **Add.**

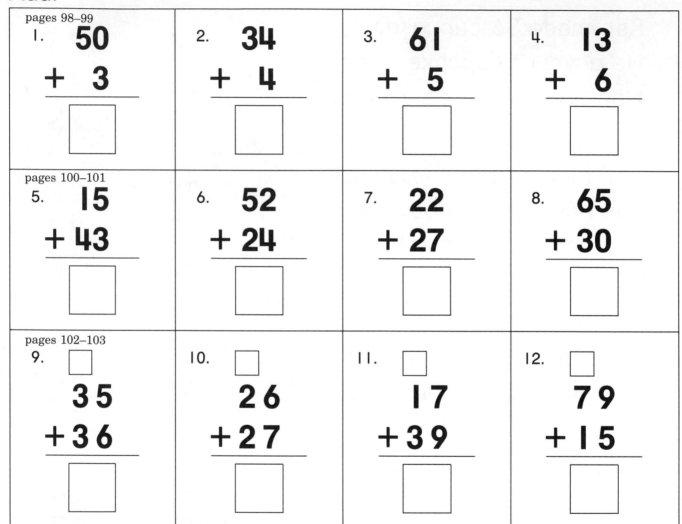

pages 98–99

1. 50
   + 3
   [ ]

2. 34
   + 4
   [ ]

3. 61
   + 5
   [ ]

4. 13
   + 6
   [ ]

pages 100–101

5. 15
   + 43
   [ ]

6. 52
   + 24
   [ ]

7. 22
   + 27
   [ ]

8. 65
   + 30
   [ ]

pages 102–103

9. [ ]
   35
   + 36
   [ ]

10. [ ]
    26
    + 27
    [ ]

11. [ ]
    17
    + 39
    [ ]

12. [ ]
    79
    + 15
    [ ]

▷ **Subtract.**

pages 104–105

13. 18
    − 3
    [ ]

14. 49
    − 4
    [ ]

15. 25
    − 5
    [ ]

16. 68
    − 2
    [ ]

▷Subtract.

pages 106–107			
17. 58 − 24 ☐	18. 37 − 27 ☐	19. 79 − 18 ☐	20. 86 − 34 ☐

pages 108–109			
21. ☐☐ 3 1 − 1 8 ☐	22. ☐☐ 5 4 − 2 7 ☐	23. ☐☐ 6 2 − 3 6 ☐	24. ☐☐ 9 7 − 6 9 ☐

▷**How much money?**   pages 110–111

25.

dollar	cents
$	.

26.

dollar	cents
$	.

▶ Ring the correct problem.

pages 112–113

27. Oscar had 63¢. He spent 22¢. How much does he have left?	63¢ + 22¢ 85¢	63¢ − 22¢ 41¢
28. Jerry has 37 white rabbits. He has 32 gray rabbits. How many does he have in all?	37 + 32 69	37 − 32 5
29. 58 students were in the park. 20 students went home. How many students are still in the park?	58 + 20 78	58 − 20 38
30. Jeff made 14 pizzas. He sold 4 pizzas. How many are left?	14 + 4 18	14 − 4 10
31. Tom picked 75 apples. Simon picked 24 apples. How many did they pick in all?	75 + 24 99	75 − 24 51

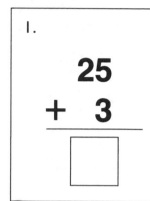

▷ Add.

1.	2.	3.	4.
25 + 3 ☐	16 +31 ☐	50 +42 ☐	☐ 1 5 +4 7 ☐

▷ Subtract.

5.	6.	7.	8.
48 − 6 ☐	89 −32 ☐	68 −20 ☐	☐ ☐ 6 1 −4 8 ☐

▷ How much money?

9.

 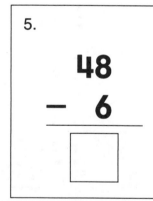

dollar	cents
	•

▶Ring the correct problem.

10.	26 students were in the library. 22 more students came into the library. How many are there in all?	$\begin{array}{r} 26 \\ + 22 \\ \hline 48 \end{array}$ $\begin{array}{r} 26 \\ - 22 \\ \hline 4 \end{array}$
11.	Angela had 45¢. She found 30¢ more. How much does she have in all?	$\begin{array}{r} 45¢ \\ + 30¢ \\ \hline 75¢ \end{array}$ $\begin{array}{r} 45¢ \\ - 30¢ \\ \hline 15¢ \end{array}$
12.	Daniel had 17 model cars. He gave 2 cars to Mick. How many does he have left?	$\begin{array}{r} 17 \\ + 2 \\ \hline 19 \end{array}$ $\begin{array}{r} 17 \\ - 2 \\ \hline 15 \end{array}$
13.	Eve made 64 doughnuts. Her class ate 33 doughnuts. How many does she have left?	$\begin{array}{r} 64 \\ + 33 \\ \hline 97 \end{array}$ $\begin{array}{r} 64 \\ - 33 \\ \hline 31 \end{array}$
14.	There were 15 bees in a garden. 14 more bees flew into the garden. How many are there in all?	$\begin{array}{r} 15 \\ + 14 \\ \hline 29 \end{array}$ $\begin{array}{r} 15 \\ - 14 \\ \hline 1 \end{array}$

Adding and Subtracting 3-Digit Numbers

▼ ▼ ▼ ▼ ▼ ▼ ▼

Dena and Tina have stamp collections. Dena has 124 stamps. Tina has 65. How many do they have in all?

Solve

▷ Make up a problem about stamps.

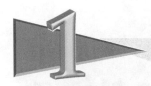

Adding Ones, Tens, and Hundreds

Step 1 Add the ones.

hundreds	tens	ones
1	2	3
+	4	1
		4

Step 2 Add the tens.

hundreds	tens	ones
1	2	3
+	4	1
	6	4

Step 3 Add the hundreds.

hundreds	tens	ones
1	2	3
+	4	1
1	6	4

Guided Practice

▷ Add.

hundreds	tens	ones
3	7	2
+	2	4
3	9	6

hundreds	tens	ones
2	4	1
+	3	6

150
+ 17

120

Practice

▷ Add.

1. $\begin{array}{r} 142 \\ + 36 \\ \hline \end{array}$	2. $\begin{array}{r} 508 \\ + 71 \\ \hline \end{array}$	3. $\begin{array}{r} 313 \\ + 85 \\ \hline \end{array}$	4. $\begin{array}{r} 724 \\ + 63 \\ \hline \end{array}$
5. $\begin{array}{r} 281 \\ + 14 \\ \hline \end{array}$	6. $\begin{array}{r} 432 \\ + 52 \\ \hline \end{array}$	7. $\begin{array}{r} 659 \\ + 30 \\ \hline \end{array}$	8. $\begin{array}{r} 815 \\ + 62 \\ \hline \end{array}$
9. $\begin{array}{r} 922 \\ + 43 \\ \hline \end{array}$	10. $\begin{array}{r} 187 \\ + 11 \\ \hline \end{array}$	11. $\begin{array}{r} 345 \\ + 31 \\ \hline \end{array}$	12. $\begin{array}{r} 422 \\ + 43 \\ \hline \end{array}$

Using Math

▷ Mary has 108 stickers.
Her brother has 81 stickers.
How many stickers do they
have in all?

They have _____ stickers in all.

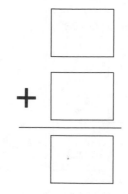

Adding Two 3-Digit Numbers

Step 1 ▸ Add the ones.

hundreds	tens	ones
1	4	6
+ 2	3	1
		7

Step 2 ▸ Add the tens.

hundreds	tens	ones
1	4	6
+ 2	3	1
	7	7

Step 3 ▸ Add the hundreds.

hundreds	tens	ones
1	4	6
+ 2	3	1
3	7	7

Guided Practice

▸ Add.

hundreds	tens	ones
4	6	3
+ 1	2	4
5	8	7

hundreds	tens	ones
6	3	5
+ 2	3	4

758
+ 120

Practice

▷Add.

1. **325** **+461** ☐	2. **836** **+132** ☐	3. **505** **+292** ☐	4. **643** **+103** ☐
5. **214** **+472** ☐	6. **786** **+111** ☐	7. **358** **+520** ☐	8. **634** **+245** ☐
9. **173** **+426** ☐	10. **717** **+130** ☐	11. **251** **+323** ☐	12. **163** **+824** ☐

Using Math

▷Carmen sold 261 boxes of Girl
Scout cookies.
Susan sold 124 boxes.
How many boxes did they sell in all?

They sold _____ boxes in all.

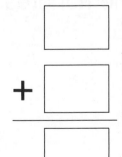

Addition with Regrouping

Step 1 Add the ones.

hundreds	tens	ones
2	6	**7**
+ 1	6	**2**
		9

Step 2 Add the tens.
6 tens + 6 tens = 12 tens
Regroup 12 tens as
1 hundred 2 tens.

hundreds	tens	ones
$\boxed{1}$		
2	**6**	7
+ 1	**6**	2
	2	9

Write the 2 in the tens' place.
Write the 1 in the hundreds' box.

Step 3 Add the hundreds.

hundreds	tens	ones
$\boxed{1}$		
2	6	7
+ **1**	6	2
4	2	9

124

Guided Practice

▷Add.

hundreds	tens	ones
1		
3	8	6
+ 2	6	1
6	4	7

← •

hundreds	tens	ones
☐		
7	9	4
+ 1	7	2

← •

☐
523
+284
☐

Practice

▷Add.

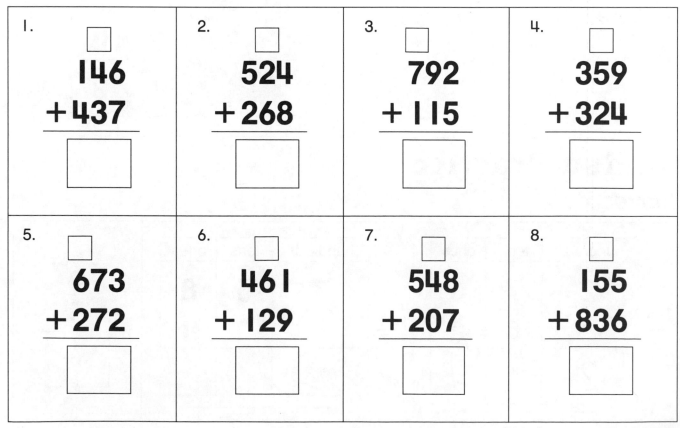

1. ☐
    146
    +437
    ☐

2. ☐
    524
    +268
    ☐

3. ☐
    792
    +115
    ☐

4. ☐
    359
    +324
    ☐

5. ☐
    673
    +272
    ☐

6. ☐
    461
    +129
    ☐

7. ☐
    548
    +207
    ☐

8. ☐
    155
    +836
    ☐

Subtracting from a 3-Digit Number

Step 1 Subtract the ones.

hundreds	tens	ones
1	3	**7**
−	2	**4**
		3

Step 2 Subtract the tens.

hundreds	tens	ones
1	**3**	7
−	**2**	4
	1	3

Step 3 Subtract the hundreds.

hundreds	tens	ones
1	3	7
− **0**	2	4
1	1	3

Guided Practice

▷Subtract.

hundreds	tens	ones
2	7	6
−	6	2
2	1	4

hundreds	tens	ones
7	5	8
−	3	4

167
− 55

Practice

▷ Subtract.

1. 486 − 52	2. 378 − 37	3. 929 − 19	4. 165 − 43
5. 591 − 50	6. 283 − 71	7. 377 − 24	8. 468 − 42
9. 759 − 33	10. 267 − 64	11. 824 − 12	12. 998 − 73

Using Math

▷ Luis had a bag with 248 pennies in it.
His bag had a hole in it.
35 pennies fell out.
How many pennies were left?

_____ pennies were left.

127

Subtracting Two 3-Digit Numbers

Step 1 Subtract the ones.

hundreds	tens	ones
3	4	6
− 2	1	3
		3

Step 2 Subtract the tens.

hundreds	tens	ones
3	4	6
− 2	1	3
	3	3

Step 3 Subtract the hundreds.

hundreds	tens	ones
3	4	6
− 2	1	3
1	3	3

Guided Practice

▷ Subtract.

hundreds	tens	ones
9	7	8
− 5	4	2
4	3	6

hundreds	tens	ones
4	8	5
− 2	5	1

$$765$$
$$-163$$

Practice

▶Subtract.

1. $\begin{array}{r} 257 \\ -132 \\ \hline \end{array}$	2. $\begin{array}{r} 586 \\ -341 \\ \hline \end{array}$	3. $\begin{array}{r} 865 \\ -723 \\ \hline \end{array}$	4. $\begin{array}{r} 628 \\ -404 \\ \hline \end{array}$
5. $\begin{array}{r} 987 \\ -684 \\ \hline \end{array}$	6. $\begin{array}{r} 396 \\ -173 \\ \hline \end{array}$	7. $\begin{array}{r} 765 \\ -514 \\ \hline \end{array}$	8. $\begin{array}{r} 479 \\ -229 \\ \hline \end{array}$
9. $\begin{array}{r} 886 \\ -343 \\ \hline \end{array}$	10. $\begin{array}{r} 547 \\ -213 \\ \hline \end{array}$	11. $\begin{array}{r} 978 \\ -746 \\ \hline \end{array}$	12. $\begin{array}{r} 685 \\ -535 \\ \hline \end{array}$

Problem Solving

▶Ring the correct problem.

86 people were on a bus.
13 people got off the bus.
How many are left?

$$\begin{array}{r} 86 \\ +13 \\ \hline 99 \end{array} \qquad \begin{array}{r} 86 \\ -13 \\ \hline 73 \end{array}$$

129

Subtraction with Regrouping

Step 1 ▶ Subtract the ones.

hundreds	tens	ones
4	3	**6**
− 2	7	**4**
		2

Step 2 ▶ Can you subtract the tens?
No. Regroup.
4 hundreds 3 tens =
3 hundreds 13 tens.
Now, subtract the tens.

hundreds	tens	ones
3	13	
4̸	3̸	6
− 2	7	4
	6	2

Step 3 ▶ Subtract the hundreds.

hundreds	tens	ones
3	13	
4̸	3̸	6
− 2	7	4
1	6	2

130

Guided Practice

▷Subtract.

hundreds	tens	ones
5	15	
~~6~~	~~5~~ 7	
− 3	8 2	
2	7	5

←——————

hundreds	tens	ones
☐	☐	
8	2 4	
− 5	3 1	

←——————

```
    ☐ ☐
  2 1 9
− 1 8 5
┌─────┐
│     │
└─────┘
```

Practice

▷Subtract.

1.
```
    ☐ ☐
  2 5 7
− 1 3 8
┌─────┐
│     │
└─────┘
```

2.
```
    ☐ ☐
  5 4 9
− 2 7 3
┌─────┐
│     │
└─────┘
```

3.
```
    ☐ ☐
  7 8 2
− 4 4 5
┌─────┐
│     │
└─────┘
```

4.
```
    ☐ ☐
  9 3 6
− 5 6 2
┌─────┐
│     │
└─────┘
```

5.
```
    ☐ ☐
  3 1 7
− 2 5 4
┌─────┐
│     │
└─────┘
```

6.
```
    ☐ ☐
  6 7 0
− 3 2 3
┌─────┐
│     │
└─────┘
```

7.
```
    ☐ ☐
  4 6 5
− 1 3 6
┌─────┐
│     │
└─────┘
```

8.
```
    ☐ ☐
  8 9 3
− 4 2 8
┌─────┐
│     │
└─────┘
```

Making Change

You have      30¢

You buy   26¢   − 26¢

Your change   4¢

Guided Practice

▷ How much change?

You have   5̶0̶¢

You buy   22¢   Your change   − 22¢   28¢

You have

You buy   80¢   Your change

132

Practice

▷How much change?

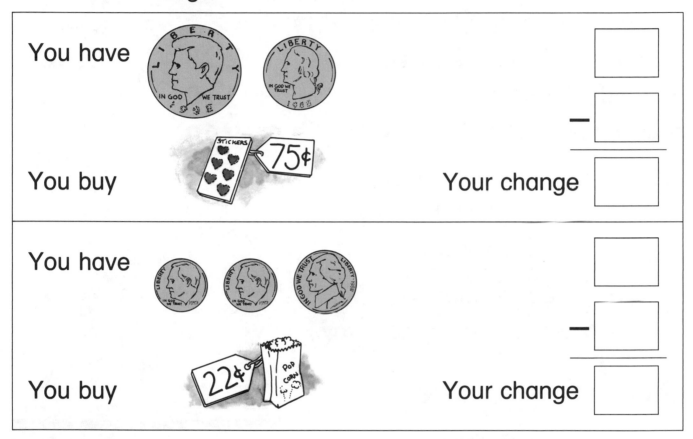

You have

You buy — STICKERS 75¢

Your change

You have

You buy — 22¢ POP CORN

Your change

Using Math

▷You have  .
Can you buy it?

49¢   **yes**   **no**   69¢   **yes**   **no**

Problem Solving

Choose an Operation

Tom had 288 tickets to sell.

He sold 110 tickets.

How many does he have left?

$$
\begin{array}{r}
288 \\
+ 110 \\
\hline
398
\end{array}
\qquad
\begin{array}{r}
288 \\
- 110 \\
\hline
178
\end{array}
$$

Tom subtracted because
he took some tickets away.
That means he now has less.

> Add to put groups together.
> Subtract to take some away.

Guided Practice

▶ Ring the correct problem.

Lisa had 167 tickets to sell. She got 31 more tickets to sell. How many does she have in all?	$\begin{array}{r} 167 \\ + 31 \\ \hline 198 \end{array}$	$\begin{array}{r} 167 \\ - 31 \\ \hline 136 \end{array}$
Bob has 312 tickets to sell. Dee has 201 tickets to sell. How many tickets do they have in all?	$\begin{array}{r} 312 \\ + 201 \\ \hline 513 \end{array}$	$\begin{array}{r} 312 \\ - 201 \\ \hline 111 \end{array}$

Practice

▷Ring the correct problem.

1.	Mrs. Smith had 123 hammers. She sold 102 hammers in one week. How many does she have left?	$\begin{array}{r} 123 \\ +102 \\ \hline 225 \end{array}$	$\begin{array}{r} 123 \\ -102 \\ \hline 21 \end{array}$
2.	There are 678 boxes of nails in a store. The store ordered 220 more boxes. How many are there in all?	$\begin{array}{r} 678 \\ +220 \\ \hline 898 \end{array}$	$\begin{array}{r} 678 \\ -220 \\ \hline 458 \end{array}$
3.	Sue got 215 boards. A day later she got 204 more. How many did she get in all?	$\begin{array}{r} 215 \\ +204 \\ \hline 419 \end{array}$	$\begin{array}{r} 215 \\ -204 \\ \hline 11 \end{array}$
4.	Tim had $526. He spent $300. How much does he have left?	$\begin{array}{r} \$526 \\ +300 \\ \hline \$826 \end{array}$	$\begin{array}{r} \$526 \\ -300 \\ \hline \$226 \end{array}$
5.	The store had 378 feet of wire. It sold 211 feet of wire. How many feet of wire are left?	$\begin{array}{r} 378 \\ +211 \\ \hline 589 \end{array}$	$\begin{array}{r} 378 \\ -211 \\ \hline 167 \end{array}$

▷ Add.

pages 120–121
1.   **346**
  + 52
 	
☐
	2. **571**
	  + 15
	
	☐
		3. **234**
		  + 44
		
		☐

pages 122–123 4. **125** **+432** ☐	5. **673** **+ 123** ☐	6. **546** **+ 242** ☐

pages 124–125
7.   ☐
    734
 + 183
 	
☐
	8. ☐
	    291
	 + 472
	
	☐
		9. ☐
		    375
		 + 261
		
		☐

▷ Subtract.   pages 126–127

10. **768** **− 32** ☐	11. **489** **− 37** ☐	12. **826** **− 13** ☐

▶Subtract.

pages 128–129		
13. $\quad$ 375 $\\ -234$ $\\$ ☐	14. $\quad$ 698 $\\ -453$ $\\$ ☐	15. $\quad$ 946 $\\ -423$ $\\$ ☐

pages 130–131		
16. ☐ ☐ $\\$ 4 3 7 $\\ -$ 1 6 3 $\\$ ☐	17. ☐ ☐ $\\$ 7 4 9 $\\ -$ 2 9 6 $\\$ ☐	18. ☐ ☐ $\\$ 5 6 8 $\\ -$ 4 8 6 $\\$ ☐

▶How much change? pages 132–133

19.

You have

You buy  32¢

Your change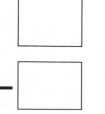

CHAPTER **6** **Review**

▶Ring the correct problem. pages 134–135

20. The student store had 275 pencils. It sold 214 pencils. How many pencils are left?	$\begin{array}{r} 275 \\ +\,214 \\ \hline 489 \end{array}$	$\begin{array}{r} 275 \\ -\,214 \\ \hline 61 \end{array}$
21. There were 356 erasers in a box. Bill put 341 more erasers in the same box. How many are there in all?	$\begin{array}{r} 356 \\ +\,341 \\ \hline 697 \end{array}$	$\begin{array}{r} 356 \\ -\,341 \\ \hline 15 \end{array}$
22. David had 420 paper clips. Koa gave David 120 paper clips. How many are there in all?	$\begin{array}{r} 420 \\ +\,120 \\ \hline 540 \end{array}$	$\begin{array}{r} 420 \\ -\,120 \\ \hline 300 \end{array}$
23. There are 683 black pens. There are 312 red pens. How many pens are there in all?	$\begin{array}{r} 683 \\ +\,312 \\ \hline 995 \end{array}$	$\begin{array}{r} 683 \\ -\,312 \\ \hline 371 \end{array}$
24. There were 184 packs of paper. Leah sold 13 packs of paper. How many are left?	$\begin{array}{r} 184 \\ +\,13 \\ \hline 197 \end{array}$	$\begin{array}{r} 184 \\ -\,13 \\ \hline 171 \end{array}$

▷ Add.

1.	2.	3.
462 + 35	724 +163	☐ 2 80 +4 38

▷ Subtract.

4.	5.	6.
675 − 41	598 −276	☐ ☐ 9 2 7 −3 6 3

▷ How much change?

7.

You have

You buy

Your change

−

▶Ring the correct problem.

8. On Monday, 486 people saw the rodeo. On Tuesday, 313 people saw the rodeo. How many people saw the rodeo?	486 + 313 799	486 − 313 173
9. There are 827 seats at the rodeo. 101 people sat in the seats. How many seats are left?	827 + 101 928	827 − 101 726
10. 162 boys rode horses one day. 40 girls rode horses that day. How many riders rode that day?	162 + 40 202	162 − 40 122
11. Bill had 465 rodeo tickets. He sold 224 rodeo tickets. How many does he have left?	465 + 224 689	465 − 224 241
12. 276 people were at the rodeo. 240 people wore boots. How many people did not wear boots?	276 + 240 516	276 − 240 36

▷Subtract.

pages 76–79

1. 11
  − 5
  ☐

2. 11
  − 9
  ☐

3. 12
  − 9
  ☐

4. 12
  − 5
  ☐

pages 80–83

5. 13 − 6 = ☐

6. 14 − 6 = ☐

7. 14 − 5 = ☐

8. 13 − 9 = ☐

9. 14 − 8 = ☐

10. 13 − 8 = ☐

pages 84–87

11. 15
  − 9
  ☐

12. 16
  − 9
  ☐

13. 18
  − 9
  ☐

14. 17
  − 8
  ☐

▷How much money?   pages 88–89

15.    ☐

Mary repairs many kinds of bicycles.
She made a graph to show how many bicycles
she repaired in one week.

Bicycles Repaired This Week

	1	2	3	4	5	6	7	8

▷ Write how many.
Add.

pages 90–91

16. + _____ in all	17. + _____ in all	18. + _____ in all
19. + _____ in all	20. + _____ in all	21. + _____ in all

142

▷ **Add.** pages 98–103

1.	2.	3.	4.
52 + 3 ☐	16 + 42 ☐	25 + 20 ☐	☐ 34 + 37 ☐

▷ **Subtract.** pages 104–109

5.	6.	7.	8.
16 − 2 ☐	38 − 28 ☐	65 − 20 ☐	☐ ☐ 53 − 26 ☐

▷ **How much money?** pages 110–111

9.

dollar	cents
$	.

▶Ring the correct problem. pages 112–113

10. Ed rode his bike 46 miles. Ming rode her bike 43 miles. How many miles did they ride in all?	$\begin{array}{r} 46 \\ +\ 43 \\ \hline 89 \end{array}$	$\begin{array}{r} 46 \\ -\ 43 \\ \hline 3 \end{array}$
11. Kelly had 58 nails. She used 30 nails to build a doghouse. How many does she have left?	$\begin{array}{r} 58 \\ +\ 30 \\ \hline 88 \end{array}$	$\begin{array}{r} 58 \\ -\ 30 \\ \hline 28 \end{array}$
12. 64 people were at the zoo. 30 more people came to the zoo. How many are there in all?	$\begin{array}{r} 64 \\ +\ 30 \\ \hline 94 \end{array}$	$\begin{array}{r} 64 \\ -\ 30 \\ \hline 34 \end{array}$
13. Emily picked 17 flowers. Elena picked 12 flowers. How many flowers do they have in all?	$\begin{array}{r} 17 \\ +\ 12 \\ \hline 29 \end{array}$	$\begin{array}{r} 17 \\ -\ 12 \\ \hline 5 \end{array}$
14. Jose had 75¢. He spent 23¢. How much does he have left?	$\begin{array}{r} 75¢ \\ +\ 23¢ \\ \hline 98¢ \end{array}$	$\begin{array}{r} 75¢ \\ -\ 23¢ \\ \hline 52¢ \end{array}$

▷ **Add.** pages 120–125

1.	2.	3.
146 + 52	763 + 123	☐ 1 9 0 + 3 7 2

▷ **Subtract.** pages 126–131

4.	5.	6.
558 − 32	465 − 234	☐ ☐ 8 6 9 − 3 8 6

▷ **How much change?** pages 132–133

7. You have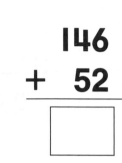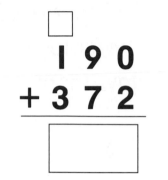

 70¢

You buy Your change

☐
− ☐
―――
☐

► Ring the correct problem. pages 134–135

| 8. | Gail made 427 loaves of bread. She sold 302 loaves of bread. How many does she have left? | 427 + 302 729 | 427 − 302 125 |

| 9. | Ed made 156 cookies for a party. Ben made 23 cookies. How many do they have in all? | 156 + 23 179 | 156 − 23 133 |

| 10. | Sid baked 288 cakes one week. Then he baked 110 more cakes. How many cakes did he bake in all? | 288 + 110 398 | 288 − 110 178 |

| 11. | A store ordered 566 cupcakes from Gail. Gail baked 423 cupcakes. How many more cupcakes does she need to bake? | 566 + 423 989 | 566 − 423 143 |

▷Add. pages 2–7

1. $\begin{array}{r} 2 \\ +\ 4 \\ \hline \end{array}$	2. $\begin{array}{r} 1 \\ +\ 3 \\ \hline \end{array}$	3. $\begin{array}{r} 5 \\ +\ 2 \\ \hline \end{array}$	4. $\begin{array}{r} 4 \\ +\ 4 \\ \hline \end{array}$

5. $7 + 0 = \boxed{}$ 6. $5 + 4 = \boxed{}$ 7. $4 + 6 = \boxed{}$

▷Subtract. pages 8–13

8. $\begin{array}{r} 6 \\ -\ 3 \\ \hline \end{array}$	9. $\begin{array}{r} 4 \\ -\ 2 \\ \hline \end{array}$	10. $\begin{array}{r} 8 \\ -\ 3 \\ \hline \end{array}$	11. $\begin{array}{r} 7 \\ -\ 2 \\ \hline \end{array}$

12. $9 - 6 = \boxed{}$ 13. $8 - 7 = \boxed{}$ 14. $10 - 2 = \boxed{}$

▷How much money? pages 14–15

15. 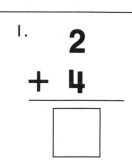 $\boxed{}$

▶**Write how many.** pages 16–17

16. _____	17. _____	18. _____
19. _____	20. _____	21. _____

▶**Write how many.**

Add.

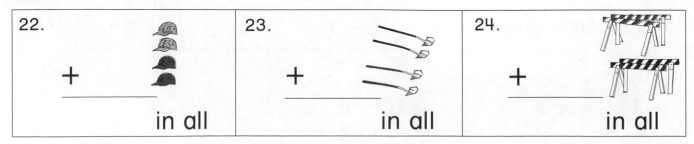

22.	23.	24.
+ _____	+ _____	+ _____
in all	in all	in all

148

CHAPTER 2 **Extra Practice**

▷**Write how many.**

pages 24–27
1.

fourteen ☐

2.

tens	ones
▯	□ □ □ □

= ☐

pages 28–31
3.

5 tens = ☐

4.

67 = ☐ tens ☐ ones

pages 32–33

5.

hundreds	tens	ones
2	7	2

= ☐

6.

hundreds	tens	ones
3	0	9

= ☐

▷**Write each missing number.** pages 34–35

7.

40		42	43

8.

298		300	

▷**How much money?** pages 36–37

9.

     ☐

149

▶**Make a drawing to solve.** pages 38–39

10. A rabbit ate 3 carrots.
It eats 2 more carrots.
How many did it eat in all?

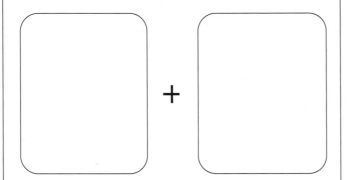

_____ carrots in all

11. Ling had 4 pennies.
Homer gave him 6 more.
How many does Ling
have in all?

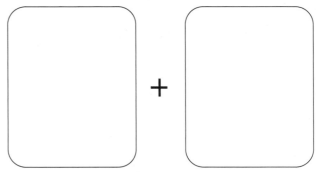

_____ pennies in all

12. Mike had 6 bananas.
He buys 2 more bananas.
How many does he have
in all?

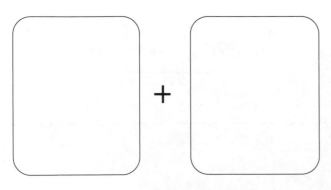

_____ bananas in all

13. Greta had 5 marbles.
Ed gave her 5 more.
How many does she
have in all?

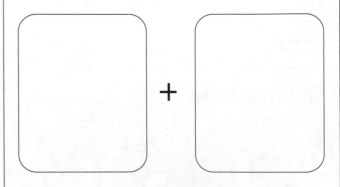

_____ marbles in all

150

▷**Add.**   pages 46–51

1. 5 $+\ 6$ ☐	2. 9 $+\ 3$ ☐	3. 2 $+\ 9$ ☐	4. 6 $+\ 6$ ☐

5. $4 + 9 =$ ☐   6. $7 + 6 =$ ☐   7. $5 + 7 =$ ☐

pages 52–57

8. 6 $+\ 8$ ☐	9. 8 $+\ 7$ ☐	10. 8 $+\ 8$ ☐	11. 7 $+\ 7$ ☐

12. $7 + 9 =$ ☐   13. $9 + 9 =$ ☐   14. $8 + 9 =$ ☐

▷**How much money?**   pages 58–59

15.  ☐

Chou works in a sewing store.
She made a graph to show what she sold.

Buttons Sold

	1	2	3	4	5	6	7	8

Type
of
Button

▶Write how many.
Add.

pages 60–61

16.	17.	18.
+ ___ in all	+ ___ in all	+ ___ in all
19.	20.	21.
+ ___ in all	+ ___ in all	+ ___ in all

Extra Practice

▶ **Subtract.** pages 76–81

1. $\begin{array}{r} 11 \\ -\ 3 \\ \hline \square \end{array}$	2. $\begin{array}{r} 11 \\ -\ 6 \\ \hline \square \end{array}$	3. $\begin{array}{r} 12 \\ -\ 4 \\ \hline \square \end{array}$	4. $\begin{array}{r} 12 \\ -\ 7 \\ \hline \square \end{array}$

5. $13 - 7 = \square$ 6. $13 - 5 = \square$ 7. $12 - 6 = \square$

pages 82–87

8. $\begin{array}{r} 14 \\ -\ 9 \\ \hline \square \end{array}$	9. $\begin{array}{r} 14 \\ -\ 7 \\ \hline \square \end{array}$	10. $\begin{array}{r} 15 \\ -\ 9 \\ \hline \square \end{array}$	11. $\begin{array}{r} 16 \\ -\ 8 \\ \hline \square \end{array}$

12. $16 - 9 = \square$ 13. $17 - 8 = \square$ 14. $18 - 9 = \square$

▶ **How much money?** pages 88–89

15. $\square$

Chen watched a parade.
The graph shows the horns he saw in the band.

Horns in the Band

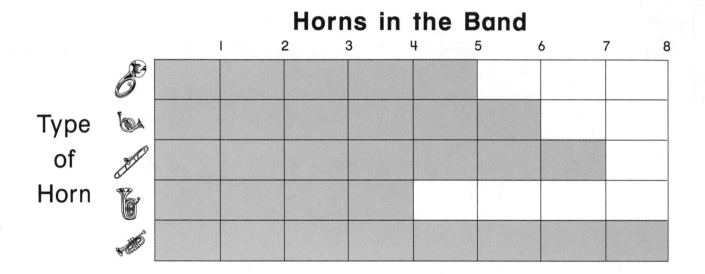

Type
of
Horn

▶ Write how many.

Add.

pages 90–91

16. 	17.	18.
+ _____ in all	+ _____ in all	+ _____ in all
19.	20.	21.
+ _____ in all	+ _____ in all	+ _____ in all

▷**Add.** pages 98–103

1.	2.	3.	4.
23 + 3 ☐	18 + 30 ☐	42 + 27 ☐	☐ 4 9 + 3 4 ☐

▷**Subtract.** pages 104–109

5.	6.	7.	8.
37 − 6 ☐	89 − 13 ☐	☐ ☐ 8 0 − 3 7 ☐	☐ ☐ 6 5 − 4 7 ☐

▷**How much money?** pages 110–111

9.

dollar	cents
$	

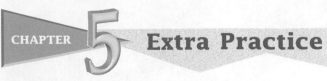

CHAPTER 5 — Extra Practice

▷ Ring the correct problem. pages 112–113

10. Beth had 65 shells. She gave 24 shells to a friend. How many does she have left?	$\begin{array}{r} 65 \\ +\ 24 \\ \hline 89 \end{array}$	$\begin{array}{r} 65 \\ -\ 24 \\ \hline 41 \end{array}$
11. Tomas had 81¢. He spent 10¢. How much does he have left?	$\begin{array}{r} 81¢ \\ +\ 10¢ \\ \hline 91¢ \end{array}$	$\begin{array}{r} 81¢ \\ -\ 10¢ \\ \hline 71¢ \end{array}$
12. Peter picked 34 oranges. Paul picked 34 oranges. How many oranges are there in all?	$\begin{array}{r} 34 \\ +\ 34 \\ \hline 68 \end{array}$	$\begin{array}{r} 34 \\ -\ 34 \\ \hline 0 \end{array}$
13. 46 children were in the pool. 23 children left the pool. How many are still in the pool?	$\begin{array}{r} 46 \\ +\ 23 \\ \hline 69 \end{array}$	$\begin{array}{r} 46 \\ -\ 23 \\ \hline 23 \end{array}$
14. In Ms. Bee's class, 17 boys can play the guitar. 12 girls can play the guitar. How many students can play in all?	$\begin{array}{r} 17 \\ +\ 12 \\ \hline 29 \end{array}$	$\begin{array}{r} 17 \\ -\ 12 \\ \hline 5 \end{array}$

▷**Add.** pages 120–125

1. 321 + 41 ▢	2. 642 +151 ▢	3. ▢ 1 8 2 + 4 3 7 ▢

▷**Subtract.** pages 126–131

5. 564 − 42 ▢	6. 487 −165 ▢	7. ▢ ▢ 7 3 5 − 5 7 2 ▢

▷**How much change?** pages 132–133

7.
You have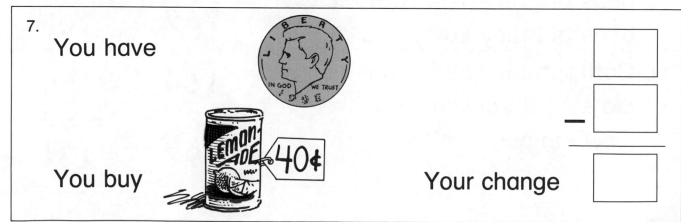

You buy

Your change

▢
▢
−
▢

▶Ring the correct problem. pages 134–135

8.	Elena stacked 326 cans of corn. She stacked 323 cans of beans. How many cans did she stack?	326 + 323 649	326 − 323 3
9.	248 customers were in the store. Then 130 customers went home. How many customers are left in the store?	248 + 130 378	248 −130 118
10.	Juan put 575 red apples out. He put 213 green apples out. How many apples are there in all?	575 + 213 788	575 − 213 362
11.	Ingrid carried 438 bags of groceries. Lou carried 331 bags of groceries. How many bags did they carry in all?	438 + 331 769	438 − 331 107
12.	Carl put out 164 gallons of milk. He sold 33 gallons of milk. How many are left?	164 + 33 197	164 − 33 131